Can
Christians
be
Saved?

A Mystical Path
to Oneness

by

Virginia T. Stephenson and Buck A. Rhodes

Dedication

This book is dedicated to Jesus and His followers and especially to those who have left their churches because of discrimination or because the dogma of their religion was interfering with their spiritual lives. This book is also dedicated to AmmaBhagavan of the Oneness University and worldwide community of Deeksha (or blessing) givers. Finally, this book is dedicated to all those who strive for the evolution of human consciousness and the end of wars.

Table of Contents

Foreword

Welcome! The journey you are about to share with Buck and Virginia is an extraordinary one, fraught with death and ecstasy, like Christ's own journey from Oneness into Oneness. Will you, the Pharisee, react violently to the raw and sensual tenderness of the authors' revelations? Will you let the authors overturn the money-changing tables in your heart, disrupting all the habits of buying and begging, selling and stealing what was always yours? Will you, like Peter, witness the authors' transfiguration, and then seek to build an altar to a new doctrine or dogma or (God forbid) a church? Or will you truly accept the authors' invitation to embrace every character in scripture as yourself, to discover the world through their eyes, and in so doing become Christ?

This book bears witness to the radical transformation that occurs when we take seriously Christ's promise that "where two or three come together in my name, I am with them." (Matthew 18:20) Before they embarked upon this journey together, Virginia and Buck had each fought hard to overcome the wounds and lies of institutional religion – in particular, of western Christianity. They had begun to discover within themselves an intimation of light and life and truth that belied the dogmas of religion. They had begun a daring and free-ranging exploration of other spiritual traditions and the truths which run like an underground river between the wells of these traditions. Finally and most importantly, they began this journey with a willingness to abandon all of these things, and to experience the scriptures with the playful innocence of children. They came together in the name of Christ, willing to discover all things anew. Virginia and Buck *lived* the scriptures in their bodies, hearts, minds, and souls . . . and in so doing, with no prior experience of the original mysteries of Christianity, rediscovered not only the way of Christ, but the beating heart of Christ in their own chests as well.

From the beginning of Christianity, you see, salvation meant not rescue, but theosis, or deification: the reawakening of God's image in each of us, and in all creation. Sin meant not failure, but the experience of separation from God. In the words of Saint Athanasius, echoed by Christian mystics throughout time, "God became human, that humans might become God." As they pursue the question, "can Christians be saved?" Buck and Virginia restored the words Christian and Salvation to their original and deepest meaning. We are "saved," or set free from the experience of separation, as we become one in Christ, the unbroken Image of God within each of us.

Buck and Virginia's sacred play also revives one of the most ancient methods for understanding scripture. Since the time of Solomon's temple, scripture was not understood primarily as literal or historical: it was understood as a beautiful garden, a paradise, or in Hebrew, *PaRDeS*. *PaRDeS* was an acronym made up of the initial letters of the Hebrew words *Peshat, Remez, Derash,* and *Sod* — four levels of understanding scripture, which together move us from a place of reading the word of God, to becoming the Word of God. The least important level, *Peshat,* is the literal or historical understanding: we relate to the characters of scripture as human beings like us, wrestling with the experience of God. The second level, *Remez,* is the allegorical understanding: every character, from Adam to Jesus, is a part of our own consciousness, and every story speaks of our internal world. *Derash* is the midrashic, intellectual, or comparative understanding, looking at patterns of meaning in the sacred teachings of the world. Finally, *Sod* is the mystical meaning, glimpsed in visions, dreams, and ceremonies. Without knowing it, Buck and Virginia reenacted all of these levels of scripture, reassembled the ancient map set forth by the mystics, and followed that map back into the Garden of Paradise, walking hand in hand with God in the Garden.

Buck and Virginia would be the first to admit that, like the great mystic Paul, "we see through a glass, darkly." (I Corinthians 13:12) This book is a faithful and courageous recounting of the journeys that brought them together, and the ecstatic journey they shared together in Christ's living presence. Since they penned the words of this book, they continue to enjoy greater revelations and deeper experiences of oneness than those revealed. What makes this book important, then, are not the particular insights they share, but the invitation to engage scripture with *your* whole being, without assumption or expectation, and the passionate determination they model to be true to *your* own experience of God. If you accept the invitation to follow Christ's invitation each moment, you can say with Christ, as Virginia and Buck have, "Behold, I make all things new." Or perhaps even more audaciously, you can pray with Christ, "As Thou, Father, art in me, and I in Thee, may they also be One in us."

Hunter Flournoy
Pastor, Amigos de Dios
Albuquerque, New Mexico 2010

Can Christians Be Saved?
A Mystical Path to Oneness

Preface

He (Jesus) but followed a precedent set by all previous World-Teachers. This god-man, thus endowed with all the qualities of Deity, signifies the latent divinity in every person. A mortal achieves deification only through at-one-ment with this divine Self. Union with the immortal Self constitutes immortality, and the person who finds this true Self is therefore "saved." This Christos, or divine in oneself, is humans' real hope of salvation—the living Mediator between abstract Deity and mortal humankind.
—Manly P. Hall[1]

Can Christians Be Saved? A Mystical Path to Oneness is a vehicle for enlightenment and awakening for all people, Christians and non-Christians alike. The issue is not our religion or lack of religion, but our view of divinity, the world, ourselves, and other people. In addition to the general Christian definition of the word *saved*, the word *saved* also means enlightened (Christed or awakened), as well as being saved from killing each other. The world may awaken to the fact that we are all brothers and sisters, whether we are a different nationality, ethnicity, or gender—and even more than brothers, ONE together in this world. We believe that this realization will save many people from their misunderstanding of divinity, which leads to the religious cycle of judgment, guilt, and fear.

The Bible is the preeminent religious text of the Western world. We use the stories from it to show that even the spiritual stories with which many of us have been familiar since our youth can bring us

---

1   Manly P. Hall: The Secret Teachings of All Ages (1928. New York, NY: Jeremy P. Thacher/Penguin, 2003), p. 583. Note: Wording altered to eliminate the sexist language of the original (1928) text.

to a truth that can override long-accepted dogma. The God that we teach throughout this book lies inside us, in our heart and soul. We have only to realize who we are to experience this divinity.

Through our years of spiritual work together, we developed a process of internalizing the Biblical stories for ourselves. This process requires interpreting the stories allegorically, not literally. An allegory is a story with a hidden meaning that gives spiritual insights. To assist the reader in understanding our process, we have interjected many personal stories into the book. Our hope is that the reader can use our process (or their own) to let these stories live in them as they have in us.

Virginia Stephenson and Buck Rhodes
Albuquerque, New Mexico, 2010

Note to the Reader

We have used four different forms of writing in this book;

I.   Regular text – This is used for most of the book. This text is telling you about this work and how you can use it.

2.   *Poetry – This is used when a primary insight first expressed itself to us as a poem. This is presented as poetry in italics.*

3.   Gestalt experiences – This is expressed in the present tense as if it is happening right now and it is how we relate our Gestalt or channeled experiences. By using the present tense, we hope that you will be better able to sense the emotional content as well as the story line of the message. This is presented as indented material using a different type to make this clear. Also the person responsible for this is given at the end. For example:

I am standing in a hallway watching a cat move slowly around the corner. He eyes are shining slits reflecting a distant light.
—Source unknown

4.   *Quotes – This is used when we have included direct information from an outside source. Usually a reference to the source is given and the author is identified. This is indented and printed in italics.*

Introduction

We began this adventure by wondering where the secrets of the ancient mystery schools were hidden. Imagine wanting to hide something very precious: these ancient rituals and dramas. Maybe you would put them in the most obvious place in the world and call them something else? We believe that this place was the Bible. And people kept the secrets well-hidden by claiming that the Bible is history: indisputable history because it is the word of God.

We both started our lives as Christians. Independently, we both were saved from fundamental Christianity in mid-life or earlier. Fear-based faith or Christian dogma became something that we simply could no longer tolerate. But when our spiritual journeys came together, we discovered a living treasure based on our personal truths. This happened when we started to experience the allegories in the Christian Bible as our own stories. By doing this, Christianity came back to life for us, presenting us with deep self-understanding like that of the initiates of the ancient mystery schools.

This process for us was greatly advanced by the teachings of Sri AmmaBhagavan of the Oneness University in Southern India. One of us, Buck, traveled first to Fiji and then to India to study Oneness after being introduced to this idea by his teacher, Arjuna[2]. Christianity and the other major fundamental Western religions, Islam and Judaism, use dualistic thinking. They teach us to think in terms of right and wrong. They conditioned us to respond automatically by making judgments and acting upon these judgments. This dualistic point of view creates separation. In the view of these religions, we all are either good or bad. We thus judge one another, as well as ourselves, and we believe that God is also judging us. Therefore, we are led to believe that God will eventually punish us unless we can be saved from what we have been taught to judge as bad in

---

2   Arjuna Ardagh: Awakening into Oneness: The Power of Blessing in the Evolution of Consciousness (Boulder, CO: Sounds True, 2007). Buck studied with Arjuna for several years and became a certified Living Essence facilitator.

ourselves. The other point of view (or the alternative to dualistic thinking) is Oneness. The idea of Oneness is that we are all one and that there is no separation. In fact, we and God are one and the same. But it takes considerable self-understanding to really get this idea, especially after being steeped in fundamentalism. But this understanding can emerge when we experience the Biblical allegories as personal stories and allow ourselves to experience the worldview of Oneness.

The inner journey begins with an awareness of where you are, not with an obsession with where you want to be.

—*Bhagavan*

The processes described in this book are designed to take you on the journey from duality to Oneness. We now believe that this is the journey that Jesus took in becoming Christ. He started out as the Son of the Old Testament God of Judgment and Punishment and finally, on the Cross, fully became the Son of the God of Love. We believe that with these processes, you, like Jesus, can become one with God, the God of Love, and as Jesus did, you will be able to say: "I and my Father are One." We have written this book because we want others to be able to benefit from these techniques to the same extent that we have.

What we are writing is **not** exegesis (a critical interpretation) of the Biblical stories, nor are we redefining the historical characters. We are relating to you our personal journeys as we experienced the stories as aspects of our Selves. This is like dreaming that we are this character and then retelling the dream as we experienced it. This is the mystical process.

What were the assumptions we thought essential to experiencing Biblical allegories personally? First, we needed to let go of the idea that the Bible is necessarily history. And second, we also let go of the idea that Jesus was necessarily a single historic character. Candidates in the mystery schools may have been referred to generically as Jesus. After personally experiencing the stories of Jesus, we realize that these assumptions about him are not important to us anymore. Although, a number of ancient gods had many attributes of the Biblical Jesus[3] and many of the sayings attributed to him were documented in earlier writings.[4] This suggests that the authors of the New Testament gave accounts of the life of Jesus that may have drawn on earlier materials. Also, they may have attributed stories or qualities to Jesus from those earlier sources. We accept the idea that the stories in the Bible are for personal use. Furthermore, we haven't accepted the principle that the Bible is the sole source of all truth. We thus open ourselves to the great truths of all sacred literature.

Another idea is that human perception and experience require acknowledging that there are polarities. For example, without light and dark, we wouldn't be able to see. So how do we deal with these obvious polarities from the Oneness point of view? We simply don't deny either pole. Basically, we accept that we are sometimes bad and sometimes good. We accept that in the dark side of us, there is much richness and power, just as there is in the other pole, or the good side. So we'll need to explore this with you, but will wait to do so until you have personally experienced some of the Biblical allegories from this new vantage point.[5]

If you are familiar with the history of early Christianity, you probably know that in the early years, there were many forms of this budding new religion. However, when the Roman Emperor Constantine decided to make Christianity the official religion of his empire, all the buds but one were pruned, and only literal Christianity was allowed to flourish. The teachers of other lines of Christian thought were killed or banished, and their writings were burned as heresy. The official church and the Roman Empire used this new religion to control their people. Jesus was voted

---

3   S. Acharya: Suns of God, Krishna, Buddha and Christ Unveiled (Kempton, IL: Adventures Unlimited Press, 2004).

4   Alvin Boyd Kuhn: Lost Light: An Interpretation of Ancient Scriptures: Filiquarian Publishing Minneapolis, Minn, 2007).

5   Please see the Three Temptations in the New Testament allegories chapter.

in as God at the Council of Nicea in 325 CE. Eventually,[6] only the pope could speak God's truth; this was the way in which the Church gave the people the dogma required for the church to maintain control of the population. Fortunately, some of the early writings have been rediscovered and translated in recent years. Important ideas from early Christianity that were intended to be hidden from us forever have now become available. Our homework before undertaking the adventure of writing this book was to study the works of the scholars who translated and wrote about these early documents. What we had discovered on our own turned out to be very similar to some early forms of Christianity revealed in those newly rediscovered documents.

The basic idea of this book is to learn by experience. This is contrary to the usual Christian doctrine: "Have faith, and believe." Christian faith results from accepting the Bible as history and as the word of God, as well as buying into the dogma put forth by church leaders. We promote the idea that our real and individual truths are only arrived at by our experiences. This is an old Christian Gnostic idea, such as that taught by Valentinus[7], one of the early teachers in the church. Some Christians begin their religious life by having faith and belief in church dogma, but because of their personal experiences, they become experientially based Christians—might you be one of them? The problem with dogmatic Christianity is that people are distracted from trusting their own experiences and mistake official dogma for their personal truth.

Knowing Jesus or other mystics occurs by personal experience. This is unlike dogma, a system of belief or doctrines handed down by high authority, such as a religious leader, especially the Catholic pope.

We contend that traditional faith-based indoctrination is not the only way, nor is it the best way to develop a personal experience of the divine and to become Christ, as Jesus did. Dogma demands of us that we believe that the Bible is historical truth. Such a belief might

---

6   A long eventuality, as the dogma of papal infallibility was not officially promulgated until the Vatican Council of 1870.

7   Elaine Pagels: The Gnostic Gospels (New York, NY: Vintage Books, 1989).

be counterproductive, nor is it required for us to believe what others teach about Jesus, Mohammed, or other mystics. When we learn from our own experiences, the learning seems to be more than just knowledge; it is experienced as wisdom.

The ultimate aim of this book is to help lead you to the personal experience of Oneness. This book is intended to nudge humanity towards inner peace, peace between nations, and protection of our earthly environment. We believe that the teachings attributed to God in the Old Testament have provided its believers with a rationale for war. War has been a constant in the history of the faith-based belief systems of the three great Western religions, Judaism, Christianity, and Islam. War after war, together with our modern destruction of the environment, create a high probability that we will destroy ourselves unless we evolve. When we discover for ourselves Oneness with the God of Love, when our consciousness becomes heart-centered rather than power-centered, the motivations for waging wars will disappear. Throughout history, human consciousness has taken several evolutionary steps. It is now time to take the next step. We hope that this book will help provide a way to do this.

Chapter 1

Our Life Journeys

Our Journeys Come Together

Virginia Speaks

First let me tell you, in the present tense (although the events happened some time ago), of a major life-changing experience.

For the past four years, I have been the pastor of a fundamentalist Christian church located next to the local university. Some of the elders of the international ministry are visiting with me. They are demanding that I get the people in my church to behave the way they want them to behave. I am to make them give ten percent of their income to the church and appear at every church event or suffer church discipline. I must confront them individually if they have sin in their lives. As I listen to this tirade, I feel disturbed. I know that the level of control that the elders are forcing me to have over my congregation is wrong. What these church leaders suggest destroys the individual's personal relationship with God and sets the leaders up as God. I cannot do what they suggest. But what am I to do? I have two small children at home, and this job as pastor is my means of support. I initially lie to them and tell them that I will do it their way, even though I have no intention of doing such a thing. But that night, as I sit with my decision, I realize that I simply cannot continue in that position under these circumstances. My resignation will be the best thing for my family, the church, and me. I am scared to lose the income, as I will have to find a job quickly, but the stress thrust upon me in being forced to pastor in a way I cannot find it in my conscience to do is intolerable. I want so much to serve God and be used by God, but I cannot do it this way. Maybe there will come another time in my life when I can lead people to the divine, but this is not the right way. I cry out to God in frustration, fear, disappointment, and regret.

—Virginia

Years later, when Buck and I had been studying together for some time, Buck postulated that perhaps the lessons and initiations of the great mystery schools were hidden in the Bible. Between the two of us, we had knowledge of most of the ancient mystery schools of the Essenes, the Egyptians, and the Golden Dawn, and both of us had in-depth knowledge of the Bible, so when we began to conduct our investigations of this book by reading parts of the Bible together, we were able to find allegorical meanings quickly. Eventually, we began to apply principles of experiential-based learning, including Gestalt analysis[8], to make the allegories even more personal and meaningful. As we internalized these personal truths into our lives, our spiritual perspective was enhanced. Rather than faith-based rules and regulations from scripture, we started reforming our lives around our newly discovered insights, our personal truths. These new insights gave rise in us to a new view of our world, one that is very different from what our original upbringing in Christianity had provided. For example, our original faith, based on the literal interpretation of the Bible, exalted Jesus as an external God who was to be worshipped, rather than a role model who pointed to truth inseparable from ourselves. The lessons and truths realized by this method changed us. We experienced the change internally as "rivers of living water." To us, Jesus now became a blesser, a healer, a forgiver, and a teacher. His greatest lesson was for us to believe that "greater works than these shall you do, because I go to the Father."[9] In other words, by being in the love-space that he taught us through His presence in our lives and our own stories and by fulfilling the initiations that were birthed within us, we began to understand that we might be able do the works that he did, and even greater works than those that he did. His experiences and stories are now ours. Jesus is no longer a distant historical Biblical character. Instead, he is in us; actually, He is us and may also be you.

Buck Speaks

I too will tell you, in the present tense (although this happened many years ago), of a major life-changing experience regarding my relationship with Christianity.

---

8   Gestalt analysis will be explained in detail in the next chapter. Frederic Pearls was the father to this approach to self-understanding and Gestalt Therapy.

9   John 14:12.

I'm a freshman in college and living away from home for the first time. My dorm room is only about half a block from the Baptist Student Union, which holds vespers services every afternoon at 5:30 p.m., half an hour after our last class. I usually walk straight from class to the vesper hall and sit there relaxing, meditating, and reflecting upon my day until the service begins. This is a great top-off to my busy day, as it allows me to regain my spirit. I attend regularly. This provides me with continuity with my life at home, where I was a very active member of the local Baptist church.

The president of the Baptist Student Union, an upperclassman, usually conducts the evening vesper service and gives a brief sermon, along with some prayers, a reading, and singing. But every once in awhile, usually before a big school dance, he will preach about the evils of dancing, about how dancing is sexually arousing and often leads to sin! Not so for me—I love dancing and have been dancing since before I entered high school. In fact, I have learned how to teach about a hundred different folk dances in addition to being good at the current type of dancing that we do at school. His anti-dancing sermons don't really bother me; his beliefs are simply different from mine on this subject. But...

one day, I am the first to arrive at the vesper service. The president of the Baptist Student Union is sitting on the steps of the building beside his girlfriend, and he has his hand up under her skirt. Our eyes meet. He quickly withdraws his hand. I whirl around and walk away, never to cross the doors of that vesper hall again. I am angry and judge him, saying almost out loud: "You hypocrite!" As I consider my response to this, I abruptly give up one of the most vital and stabilizing activities of my life as a new college student and later will become self-critical because of this decision. This judgment spread from that moment to include many others whom I had observed as a Christian living contrary to what I had heard them preaching to me.

—Buck

Years later, Virginia and I started meeting together on a weekly basis for meditation, followed by a spontaneous discussion of whatever would come up. As Virginia mentioned above, one day, the hypothesis came up that the Gospels were the secret hiding place of the teachings of the ancient mystery schools.

This was a fortunate synchronicity because years earlier, after learning about how important the initiations of the Elysian school were for some of the greatest men in history, I decided to discover the basis for the teachings of these schools. This current hypothesis came after reading Whitworth's book *The Nine Faces of Christ*.[10] This book describes the initiations of Joseph-bar-Joseph (who was probably Jesus). This Jesus was an Essene. When he finished this training, he then proceeded to undergo a series of nine advanced initiations, including a death and resurrection ritual.

This hypothesis so inspired us that we challenged ourselves to explore this idea about the connection between the Gospels and the ancient mystery schools. We started reading the Gospels together as if they contained allusions to hidden, ancient teachings. Each allegory we studied in this manner provided us with surprising new insights into our lives, truths that supplanted the dogma that we had previously rejected. This approach helped us to find significant new personal meanings in each of the Gospel stories that we explored.

---

10 E. E. Whitworth: Nine Faces of Christ: Quest of the True Initiate (Marina Del Ray, CA: Devorss Publications, 1980).

However, one thing began to puzzle us. In some of the passages attributed to Jesus, Jesus speaks of love and forgiveness. In other passages, Jesus speaks judgmentally, as when he gets angry at the fig tree (when it doesn't have any figs for him and his disciples when they are hungry). So he kills the tree! This led us to a further idea that the Gospels present the stories of at least two distinct representations of Jesus: one who is the (metaphorical) son of the Old Testament God and the other the son of the God of Love, the God introduced in the New Testament.[11] Perhaps the Gospels are the story of the evolution of Jesus from representing the Old God to becoming a representative of the New God.

At first, the Gospels then appeared to us as a confused mixture of two contrary underlying philosophies: oneness and duality. So then we became cautious in our reading, bypassing the sayings of Jesus when he speaks as the son of the Old Testament God. We began to understand this more clearly when we reexamined the Creation story in the beginning of the Old Testament (the Book of Genesis),[12], reading it as a teaching allegory and asking ourselves what this story actually teaches the two of us at this point in our lives. The result brought a lot of things together, especially for me, as I was already deeply into the study of Oneness.

Our new realizations about the story of Adam and Eve in the Garden of Eden really stimulated our enthusiasm for this way of Bible study. We will report in the following chapters on several major adventures and sets of new realizations. Also, we began to consider other sacred literature as we were now considering the Bible. Teaching allegories and patterns for initiations are widely available in most sacred writings.

Individual Journeys – Virginia Speaks

I was raised in the home of a Baptist minister. I remember my father as a loving man, although he saw the world in a very fixed and

---

11 Perhaps a more plausible explanation of this is that the writers of the Gospels were confused by these two different views of God.

12 This story is fully explored in Chapter 3: Old Testament Allegories

rigid way. Nonetheless, he never underestimated the power of love. I so admired him that it took me many years to find my own spiritual way independent of him as an influential role model. By wanting to emulate him, I could not see another path.

During my school years, I participated in all the church activities expected of Southern Baptist children, and I saw all the flaws, inconsistencies, and hypocrisies in the people in the church, which made me wonder how these things could be. Why was religion not able to help people to overcome these things? All of my friends and community were in the church, so breaking away was not a real option for me. When I left for college, that was another story. I immediately starting drinking and taking drugs. I partied my way through college, but graduated in spite of myself. During college, however, I could not give up religion and practiced Zen Buddhism for several years, an experience that I will never forget.

After graduating from college, I continued to do drugs, but I moved back to my hometown, and although I lived apart from my father, I still felt his influence in my life. So several years after graduating, I went to the altar at his church, had a born-again experience, and gave my life "back to God." This included my giving up drugs. As I now had a testimony[13] and a good ability for public speaking, very soon thereafter, I found myself as the pastor of a small nondenominational church. Serving in that capacity soon led me to participate in a larger ministry to colleges on several campuses in the U.S. I pastored a church on a college campus in New Mexico for four years until the pressure from the hierarchy of the church became greater than the joy of helping others there.

One of the things that continually bothered me was the statement by the church elders that AIDS was God's punishment for gays. This always bothered me because the God that I knew, who sent his Son to die for the sins of humanity, would not send an Old Testament plague to punish sinners in our time. We were under a

---

13 A testimony is a public profession of a religious experience. It usually fits the form of "That is what I used to be, but I have been changed by God, so now I am this way."

Can Christians be Saved?

New Covenant of Love, and I knew that the church's condemnatory way of thinking was harmful and destructive. The few times when I started to mention this to my superiors, I was warned to keep that thought to myself. One time, a group of my superiors came to me and told me that I had a demon of homosexuality, and they prayed over me for several hours in an attempt to cast it out. I submitted to them and tried to be humble and open to them, but in my heart, I knew that they were wrong and that the God that I knew was having none of the charade that was playing out before me. So after a few months of hell on earth, I left the ministry, as I explained above. I felt a great relief at being free.

Several years later, my spouse and I divorced after nineteen years of marriage. I finally gave myself permission to ask myself why I had always felt so different from other men. I thought that this feeling of differentness must be because I was gay; maybe those church elders had been right. So I started attending a church in Albuquerque that welcomed gays and lesbians. I found a wonderful congregation of people who were gay and lesbian who loved God and were seeking the truth of life. At this church, my faith-based Christianity began its transition to experienced-based Christianity. By confronting the verses in the Bible that seemed to condemn gays and lesbians and seeing that these verses did not apply to homosexuals today, I became free to see that the words of the Bible were guideposts and not literal commandments. After being in that church for several years, I saw that life and spirituality were bigger than any book or man-made God, so I began to seek a wider and deeper experience of spirituality.

I began to study and practice many other religions and philosophies. I read all the sacred texts that I could find, such as numerous Buddhist texts, the *Upanishads*, the *Bhagavad Gita*, and Vedic writings. My readings included the more esoteric works, such as those used in the *Kabbalah*, Sufism, and pagan disciplines. My love of Buddhist thought returned, and as I quickly regained my old practice, I realized that I was experiencing a dying to the attachments in my life, such as money, a job, comfort, reputation, and cultural approval. As I shed my attachments to those things, I regained a new appreciation of the joys of life.

14

The many fears that I faced served to help me to lose my attachment to the things that I feared to lose. At that time (2001), I was a manager at a Fortune-100 private company. I knew that many people would condemn my decision to make a major change in my life (which will be discussed later) or would be unable to understand it. I also knew that I could very well lose my job and the financial security that it provided. Walking through the fears, adversity, and loss of things allowed me to see what was truly important in life and to be thankful for who I am.

In this experience of confronting and releasing my fears, I was finally able to see the divine as experience-based, to realize that the purpose of religion is self-discovery and affirmation. I realized that the great religions of the world should serve the purpose of personal enrichment and discovery. What they have become today, unfortunately, is organizations of group control with faith-only foundations. Nevertheless, as I look back on the early years of my life, I am still thankful for my father. Although I do not follow his specific path, I follow his belief that my relationship with the Divine is the most important thing in life. His experience of that relationship with the Divine lives within me as my experience.

My spiritual path today has evolved into a wonderful mix of several disciplines, religions, and philosophies. Buddhism is my core practice. Oneness, a concept explained in the next chapter, is consistent with Buddhist thought. Mindfulness, nonjudgment, and impermanence: are all excellent spiritual practices and ways of thinking. I also am a member of a Druid grove, where we practice the ancient religion of the Celts. This involves a celebration of ritual and states of higher consciousness. I also am a member of the Mountain Lodge, a wonderful collection of friends who practice Native religion, as well as shamanism and ritual.

This book is a detailed explanation of the journey that Buck and I have taken into mystical Christianity. Along with my other spiritual endeavors, this delving into mystical Christianity has also become an integral part of my life.

Individual Journeys: Buck Speaks

"Believe, or go to Hell!" This was imprinted into my young mind by Baptist ministers during my childhood. I eventually rejected Christian dogma. Hell was simply unbelievable to me. Yet I did have personal experiences that have convinced me that Jesus or other Christ-conscious figures can be personal guides, as defined by Gary Zukav.[14] Jesus loves me, not because the Bible tells me so, but because I have experienced that love.

As a beginning college student (as explained above), I gave up Christianity, but I never forgot that God is love or that a divine presence is always available to me.

After graduating from college, getting married, serving through the military in the Public Health Service, having a daughter, going to graduate school, writing my doctoral dissertation, getting a divorce, and becoming a faculty member and researcher, I began to explore religion again, this time as a Unitarian. I helped to organize a human relations seminar at the Unitarian Church in Baltimore. The group morphed into an encounter group. Because of what we did in this group, I discovered that I could actually have feelings. After about a year in this group, I finally got enough insight and courage to admit that I was gay. As a result of what I experienced and learned in the encounter movement, I became interested in more deeply exploring a spiritual path. This became a major part of my life and motivated me to explore many different avenues.

In my professional life, I became a full professor with tenure, first at the University of Kansas and then at the University of New Mexico in Albuquerque, where I've lived since 1976. I started a gay church in Albuquerque and became the faculty advisor of the Gay and Lesbian Student Association, which allowed its members to move onto the campus as an official university organization. My professorships were in the School of Medicine (Radiology) and the School of Pharmacy (Nuclear Pharmacy). However, when I spoke out on a local TV news program against Proposition 6 (known as the Briggs Initiative),

---

14 Gary Zukav: The Seat of the Soul (1989. New York, NY: Simon and Schuster, 1990), p. 100.

a proposed California law that would cause gay teachers and their supporters to be fired, I too was fired. Even though I had tenure, these TV interviews resulted in my being fired as Professor of Radiology from the University of New Mexico. Fortunately, my other professorship, the one in the College of Pharmacy, did continue. Nevertheless, I was still discriminated against by some of the senior faculty members. I soon left the University. I entered the field of biotechnical research and eventually became president of my own company.

As I got close to retirement, I became a certified hypnotherapist and then an ordained minister of the Living Essence Foundation. I still routinely perform hypnotherapy and serve as a minister through the Foundation.

Something had happened to me at the end of the 1970s that was profoundly influential. I made a major career change by leaving the University and going into industry. To help find my way through all these changes, I decided to take the advice of a close friend and do psychosynthesis with Walter Polt. When he asked what I wanted to do, I explained that I didn't have a plan except to give myself the gift of self-exploration. He then asked, "What comes to your mind as you say that?" Two things came up: (1) some strange, inexplicable things that happened to me during childhood, and (2) I always wanted to play the drum. (He had a drum sitting in plain sight.) So he handed me the drum and said, "Play." I did. As I played the drum, I started to have a vision. Four old Native American grandfathers approached and began speaking to me. Walter took notes of what they said. When the trance was over, I was totally amazed. Their teachings were awesome.

Week after week, Walter and I continued this. By the third week, I had obtained a recorder and began to transcribe the drumming trances. Eventually, I stopped working with Walter, but I continued the weekly sessions with just the drum and the recorder. I recorded about 200 sessions. The sessions included several classical shamanistic initiations, although I didn't appreciate this fact until later when I studied shamanism. Because of this series of experiences, I became very familiar with the spirit world. I became a student of shamanism and eventually a practitioner.

Can Christians be Saved?

About three years ago, my interest in Christianity returned due to my reading books that documented the early days of Christianity. These writings were mostly the ones that debunk teachings of the Roman Catholic Church and other fundamental Christian denominations and provide evidence that the Bible does not present history, but teaches through allegories. Many of these books report studies that show that most of the teachings attributed to Jesus were known well before his time. Recently, many have explored facets of Christianity ignored by modern fundamental Christianity. One such book that made a huge impression is *Nine Faces of Christ*.

One outcome of my later studies has been the realization that in my judging the Baptist Student Union president, I could not see who he really was, nor who I really was. I saw (or judged) only his hypocrisy, which I now see as a reflection of my own hypocrisy. I did not see that he was trying to deal with the conflict between the desires being generated by his emerging male sexuality and his belief system, which condemned his feelings as sinful. To him, just as to me, his natural sexual feelings were a bad thing, a sin. His sermons were directed more at himself than at anyone else and really had little to do with me. By judging him, however, I was the one who lost something sacred. I have finally realized how judging someone else is simply a reflection back on self. In this case, this resulted from a belief about God that I no longer hold to be true.

Within the last two years, I started to explore Oneness, going first to Fiji to study and then to India, where the Oneness University originated. These experiences began to bring all my previous studies into an overall and harmonious system. The Oneness training taught me to look for God inside myself and emphasized that this is to be experienced as a presence rather than as an intellectual concept. During the time leading up to this, I had been reading extensively about early Christianity, but certainly hadn't returned to believing that Christianity was a religion that I wanted to practice. However, the Oneness training opened me up to creatively reexploring Christianity.

✳✳

Chapter 2

Allegorical Interpretation: Process and Methods

We are at Ten Thousand Waves, a Japanese-style spa in Santa Fe, New Mexico, for the ritual of baptism. Virginia is John the Baptist; Buck is being baptized. When lifted from the water, Buck is filled with the memory of his first baptism and begins speaking to the Rev. Green, the Baptist minister who raised him the first time from the baptismal waters. Virginia immediately switches from John the Baptist to Rev. Green. Buck, for the first time in his life, has the opportunity to explain to the Rev. Green how he truly felt as a result of that original baptism:

> I didn't really want to be baptized, but I also didn't want to feel like an outsider in our church. Neither you nor anyone else ever offered me the chance to tell my truth. I was dishonest in agreeing to this baptism and now I wish I hadn't agreed

to it. But I don't blame you for my mistake. Please forgive me for being dishonest.

—Buck as a boy

Rev. Green, in the form of Virginia, offers Buck an apology for not listening to him and accepts his request for forgiveness. An old wound has been healed, a wound that Buck didn't even know he had been carrying. This is an example of character assumption, a technique that we often use in this Gestalt work. Usually, each of us assumes that he or she is a character in the allegory on which we are working.

After we had agreed to explore the idea that the wisdom of the ancient mystery schools could be excavated from their hidden places in the Bible, we excitedly began this adventure. One technique that we use is to read each story as if it is actually about us and our lives. When one of us gets a personal insight into a story, this could inspire a similar or entirely different insight in the other. After hearing the other's insight, we often get additional revelations about ourselves. Thus, the method emerged of reporting our experiences as done in chapter I: Virginia speaks, then Buck speaks, and then Virginia speaks again, etc.

As we progressed with these role-playing exercises, we began to define and improve our methods for the allegorical interpretation of these Biblical stories. Becoming a character and enacting that character became one of our main tools. We also incorporated other important tools, including Gestalt analysis and ritual enactment.

Buck Describes Gestalt Analysis

Gestalt[15] analysis happens when a sacred story is told as if it is happening right now and is the storyteller's very own story. For example, Virginia became Jonah in the Old Testament allegory of Jonah and the Whale. As Jonah, she described her inner conflicted

---

15 Claudio Naranjo: *The Techniques of Gestalt Therapy* (Highland, NY: Gestalt Journal, 1980).

feelings when God gave her the command to go to Nineveh and preach to the people there. At each step of the story, she continued telling it in the present tense and revealing to me, the listener/coach, just what she was experiencing. And when she happened to slip into reporting in the past tense, I'd stop her and ask her, in my role as coach, to repeat what she had just said, but in the present tense. As the listener of the story, I heard her expressing the same fears at each step of the story. For example, she'd express the fear that God would punish her if she didn't do as God demanded, along with the fear that the people of Nineveh would punish her if she did go and do what God wanted her to do. She expressed a fear of the storm that she experienced while on the boat, and the fear that the other passengers on the boat would throw her overboard. She feared death inside the whale's belly. Basically, the story revealed that she could not run away from her fear. And the lesson for her was that when she faced her fear, things turned out well.

More on the Use of the Gestalt Technique

I am the waters of the River Jordan. I flow over a crossing of the river where people often gather. A rather earthy fellow comes here to do the ceremony called baptism. He says prayers and then dunks people into me. I can feel them undergoing a change; their energy shifts, and I am able to wash something out of them that they don't want as a part of themselves anymore. When they are raised out of me, the onlookers seem to experience a greater level of joy. And the ones who have been raised seem to have a new and more powerful intention for their life.

A man arrives at my shore and speaks to the Baptist, the one who does the baptizing. The Baptist knows this man, but is unsure what to do with him. But this man, whom the Baptist refers to as Jesus, insists upon receiving the baptismal rites. When they walk into the water, I immediately know that something unusual is happening because there is a light around these two, and the light even penetrates into me. I've never felt so powerful before. Instead of something being washed away from this man, this light that is all around and within me washes into him. I too, bless this man. I, too, love this man. I too, know a hope that I've never known before. The joy around me has never been so great.

—Buck as the Jordan River

The Gestalt technique requires the insertion of ourselves into each of the characters and sometimes even into a substance or object that appears in the story. This technique also utilizes a listener who can also serve a dual role as coach. To do Gestalt work, we became the person or object and tell the story, using the present tense. This requires our imagining that we actually experience the story right now. In particular, we experience the feelings that go along with the progression of the events, and we report our feelings aloud to the listener. This is best done with another who listens to us while imagining being there with us. Sometimes, it is advantageous for the listener to assume the role of a specific character. For example, Buck often wants to tell his story to Sophia, the Goddess of Divine Wisdom, so he asks Virginia to become this goddess. Careful attention is given to the feelings as they emerge and are told to the listener. Frequently, at a specific point in the story, a major insight arises. For example, you may get an instant replay of a set of feelings from a past event in your life. Sometimes, a single telling of the story in this manner is sufficient to get your personal meaning from the allegory. At other times, several of the characters may need to be explored in this manner until the insight comes.

Gestalt means to get the overall or big picture, the synthesis. This is achieved by experiencing and inhabiting the parts of the story as it is retold, over and over, in the present tense. This process continues until an ah-ha experience is achieved. The listener is our coach, who keeps us from going into the past tense, which would cause the story to get lost as a memory rather than remaining as a vital right-now experience. For example, to **understand the baptism of Jesus, it is necessary to BE Jesus, to be the dove,**[16] to be the baptizer, and to be the water or the Jordan River. This way of relating the story continues until a sudden realization is achieved as to how the story relates to our own life. In other words, we apply the story to ourselves experientially. The coach may also get insights about which character should tell the story next or which object or space would be useful to become the storyteller. For example, when Virginia was telling the story of Jonah and the Whale, if she hadn't gotten the big picture yet, as coach, I might have asked her to become the whale and to explain the story to Jonah as he was in its belly.

At times, dreams will come to us, bringing additional insights into our interpretations. For example, Buck's initial Gestalt approach to the allegory of the baptism of Jesus was done alone late at night after he had gone to bed.[17] In the midst of the process, he fell asleep, but he continued the story in the dream. This dream-story revealed life-changing information, which probably would not have been encountered otherwise.

Gestalt dream analysis[18] is also a recommended technique, especially if the interpretation of the dream is not directly realized. This is done the same way, that is: retelling the dream over and over in

---

16 Buck's sister, when she was baptized at the age of ten, felt the hand of God on her shoulder when she came up out of the water. And still today, she has a very vivid memory of the warm feeling of God's hand blessing her in that way. She has remained a faithful Christian since that life-changing moment. If this had been analyzed by Gestalt, the dove might have symbolized the hand of God.

17 Although we suggest doing Gestalt with another person, it is possible to do this alone after a little practice.

18 Buck Rhodes: Helping *Others Analyze their Dreams* (previously unpublished manuscript). This method was originally learned in the late 1960s and has been employed many times during the intervening years. See Appendix 5.

the present tense as each character or object in the dream. Often, a major insight happens when the dream is told as the container of the dream. For example, the final telling of a baptism dream might be as the Jordan River (or whatever was the site of the dream). In this example, the person might ask the Jordan River to explain to the dreamer why this dream was given to him or her.

Channeling is a term that is sometimes used interchangeably with the term *character assumption* in our storytelling. In our telling of allegories, we may assume that we are experiencing the story as a specific character in the story. We do this in the present tense, just as with Gestalt dream analysis. Thus we give ourselves the privilege of experiencing the character as if we really were this character. You will find an example of this in the case in which Virginia tells the story of Abraham and Isaac as the angel who points out to Abraham that he can substitute the ram caught in the bush for Isaac. Others often use the word *channeling* to indicate being possessed by a spiritual entity, such as the Archangel Michael. In either case, there is a shift in consciousness to a state that is fully alert yet dreamlike and often gives a vivid experience of the character and new insights into the meaning of the allegory.

Rituals have given us some of our most powerful experiences. The Bible is rich with stories that can become very powerful rituals, for example feet washing and the Last Supper. In fact, the Penitentes[19] of New Mexico still reenact the Crucifixion ritual of the New Testament every Easter with one of their members given the honor of playing the role of Jesus.

The key to converting an allegory into a ritual or drama is to look into the story to discover within yourself what you need to empty (*kenosis* = self-emptying) and what you need to fill (*plenosis* = self-filling). For example, if you decide to use the story of Jesus washing the feet of his disciples, you might begin by asking yourself what you need to empty out of yourself to do this. As Jesus, you probably will have to empty out something different from what you would need to empty as a specific disciple. If we are too proud to let God wash our feet, as Peter was, then we've gotten the clue that

19 http://southwest.library.arizona.edu/spmc/body.I_div34.html

we need to let go of pride. This can then become one of the intentions of our ritual. Then we also need to ask what we need to be filled with. Perhaps, as was the case with Jesus, we might need to fill ourselves with the desire to serve others. Or maybe we will need to fill ourselves with humility. The best intention is the one that truly fits us personally.

With these processes, we also seek to receive the truths that are beyond the literal, truths that are specific to our own journeys and life experiences. We would ask ourselves questions such as: "What does the dove in the story of the baptism of Jesus actually symbolize to me personally?" Or "Is there an explanation in this story for events in our past?" For example, if there is a death in the story, we ask ourselves what part of ourselves died.

What we didn't do at first, but now wish that we had done from the beginning, was to tape-record our sessions. This would have been a great help because at times, we become so involved in the story that we remembered it later more like a dream than a waking experience. Some key parts may remain hidden in our subconscious. Having a witness, namely each other, has been very helpful to us in recalling our experiences.

In summary, we have used a combination of techniques to get at each allegory's personal meaning for each of us: (1) relating the story to ourselves by assuming that we are a character in the story. Thus the story becomes about our personal lives and experiences; (2) making a Gestalt analysis of the story; (3) dreaming about the story; (4) channeling a character in the story; and (5) making the story into a ritual or drama involving us individually, together, and sometimes with a group.

One of the great teachings of Bhagavan of the Oneness University is: "Anything fully experienced turns into joy." An example of this was Virginia's intense suffering as she lost everything in her descent into hell in the death-resurrection experience.[20] She was suffering not only for herself, but also for all of her sisters who had gone through the same transition. When this experience was completed,

---

20 This story is told in detail later in this book. See chapter 5.

she had emptied out her suffering and could truly experience the joy of being filled with the presence of the Divine.

> *"We are invited to forget ourselves on purpose, cast our awful solemnity to the winds, and join in the general dance."*

—*Thomas Merton*

Plenosis is what happens during the filling time after kenosis or emptying. This needs keen attention to discover a deeply longed-for intention. Making this effort can fill ourselves with either our true desire or with junk. A ritual that starts with an emptying creates an inner space that needs to be filled. Taking the time before the ritual to discern exactly what it is that we want and setting the intention to receive this can result in a positive benefit. The great example is the death of Jesus on the Cross, which was an act of emptying himself from being dominated by the God of Judgment, while the Resurrection was filling himself with the God of Love.

Part of the energy for this work derives from the trust, understanding, and respect that we have for each other. There is no need to question or doubt the response in each other or to doubt whether all is being said. But we do challenge each other and ask questions to help each other get to the core of our understanding. If we think that we can assist the other in his or her life, we speak up. By doing this together, we live the stories together, and the experience becomes a journey of reflection, revelation, and transformation.

So as we explain the stories and relate to you our experiences, we give this to you as it happened to us. We tell stories from our past, we share with you our poetry, and we tell of our experiences with dreams. We tell you of the crises in our lives and how they have blessed us. We speak of the accomplishments of our lives and how they revealed to us their real meaning only later.

The Underpinnings of this Methodology

There are some basic ideas behind these methods and processes.

An old belief is like an old shoe.
We so value its comfort that we fail to notice the hole in it.

—*Robert Brault*

Convictions are more dangerous enemies of truth than lies.

—*Friedrich Wilhelm Nietzsche*

Basic Underlying Idea Number 1: **Believing is a block!** If we believe that we have lost our keys, then we can look directly at them, but not see them. Our belief blocks our seeing. If we believe that Jesus is God and that he is in heaven, he may be talking to us in an inner voice simply as a friend, but we may not be able to hear Him. If we believe that heaven is a reward for living life according to certain beliefs given to us and that this reward is given after death, then we cannot experience the Kingdom of God right now in our lives as Jesus said that we could. It is good to know what we believe so that we can realize what our minds are filtering out of our conscious experience. For example, many or most people believe that war is inevitable, and we seem always to be at war.

"I don't have to have faith; I have experience."

—*Joseph Campbell*

Basic Idea Number 2: **Trust our own experiences!** Jesus did not follow the doctrines laid down by the leaders of his own religion. Buddha would have died before he became a great teacher if he had not stopped doing what others were showing him to do. After failing in various ascetic practices, he did not give up. "Henceforth, he would rely on his own insights."

Even though we tend to forget this, actually we do already know how to trust our own experiences. Didn't we learn not to touch a hot stove by touching one? Someone's telling us not to was simply unbelievable until we had our own blistering experience. So why do so many of us rely on others to tell us how to live our lives and to determine for us what is right and wrong? We were often told: "Just believe by faith!" The Christian challenge has often been to "take it on faith." By faith alone, we are supposed to believe others' interpretation of the Bible. If we don't, we are threatened with being sent to hell after we die. Isn't this a clever gimmick to get us to mistrust our own experience? Christianity has made faith, rather than experience, sacred.

The ancient mystery schools, including the Egyptian, Eleusinian, and Dionysian schools, used learning by experience as their method. Their exact methods were so highly respected by their successful candidates that they agreed to maintain them as secret so as not to limit their utility for future students. We learn from the writings of the students of these schools that what they learned transformed their lives, but we don't know exactly what they experienced. However, our experiences show us that these secret truths can be revealed when we relive them.

> *Outside ideas of right doing and wrong doing, there is a field.*
> *I'll meet you there.*

> —*Rumi*

> *To know a thing is to distinguish it from everything else.*
> *To forget these distinctions is to become aware of undifferentiated unity*
> *and to lose all sense of being a separate individual.*

> —*Yan Hui, a student of Confucius*

Basic Idea Number 3: **Avoid dualism that separates** us from ourselves, others, and the divine. Unconscious decision-making results in dualism. Thus dualism has become the basic operating principle embedded in most of our minds. If you are like most people, you are probably totally unaware that you ever made the decisions that resulted in your being dualistic in your thinking. This way of experiencing our world was given to us by our culture, our families, and yes, the Christian, Jewish, and Muslim religions, even if we never attended a church, a synagogue, or a mosque.

Dualism operates insidiously within ourselves. We may do something that our culture has labeled as wrong or bad, and we then start to judge ourselves. We split ourselves into the bad person and the judge, characters who are at odds or war with each other. We are likely do to this without ever stopping to think about it; we do it automatically.

When we judge others, we make ourselves separate from them. Then, instead of walking "in their moccasins," we are more likely to be "stepping on their toes." Furthermore, judgments usually result in shaming and punishing. Sometimes the outcome is killing. And when we extend this behavior to cultures or countries the outcome is often war.

Dualism also separates us from the divine, from God or consciousness. The figure of Jehovah, the God of the Old Testament, is the example of our belief that God is "out there," not inside us. We have believed that God "out there" is Holy, whereas we are not. We have fragmented and compartmentalized God out of our Spirit.

Our Western churches have taught dualism mostly in the form of sin, judging good versus evil. We will show later in the book how this dichotomy was subtly pointed out in the story of the Garden of Eden and how the focus on good versus evil has become the root of much conflict within ourselves and in the world. This collective mindset is not serving humanity well. It keeps getting us into wars. It makes us careless about our environment and is the source of much unhappiness. We have become so focused on this mindset that we forget the alternative, oneness, which is the surrender of dualism.

In many situations, oneness is a more appropriate mindset. Embracing oneness results in our lives and our world being much better off.

Oneness Compared with Dualism

Oneness is a state of spirituality in which there is no separation. There are no individual parts because all is one. The fact that I see me as a separate body from you is an example of being in the state of dualism. Believing that you and I are one is oneness. If you and I are one, then I will love you as I love myself, and I will respect you and have compassion for you, as I do myself. I will not judge you as better as or worse than I am because we are one.

If we look for an explanation of oneness, then we see that each person has a higher self, a divinity, and this higher self as it exists in every person is the same. If we consider that we are one with all sentient beings, meaning those with consciousness, then it becomes impossible for us to wage war or to harm anyone.

The realization of oneness has been called enlightenment or awakening. We might now also refer to this as being saved. A person who lives in oneness practices nonjudgment because that is the nature of oneness. Compassion and love are the motivations of a life lived in oneness, and beauty is seen in everything, not just in cultural stereotypes. A person who lives in oneness observes and watches the world, creating solutions for the challenges presented in living.

Oneness makes being with persons we know very special, and oneness makes being with strangers an exciting opportunity to touch the divine in them and be touched by them. True peace is found in oneness because stress and striving are not there. Striving is experienced because of comparisons with others or with an ideal, while in oneness, there are no comparisons.

Individual beliefs and dogma are found in dualism, not in oneness. If I am a Christian, I am at one with the Buddhist; if I am a Democrat, I am at one with the Republican. If I am one with all, I allow and honor all others to be on their own paths, although these might differ from mine.

Allegorical Interpretation: Process and Methods

The time will come when the secret wisdom shall again be the dominating religious and philosophical urge of the world. The day is at hand when the doom of dogma shall be sounded[21].

—*Manly P. Hall*

In oneness, there is no dogma. My oneness nature means that I value others as I value myself, and in this, there is a wonderful presence of natural morality that loves, honors, and respects all.

Many of us have been instructed during our religious upbringing to have compassion and love for others. Nonetheless, as we observe our world, we often find that this instruction is not as widely practiced as would be expected if we were all following our training. Oneness has provided us with the idea that we begin with a practice of having compassion for ourselves. Then if we can have compassion for ourselves, will we not more easily learn to have compassion and love for others? When we learn to experience both, then we are experiencing oneness.

I'm sitting in a room with about 30 other people at the Oneness University in India. A young, warm, vigorous man, a dasha as they are called here, is talking to us about compassion for ourselves. He invites us to remember the self-judgments, shame, guilt, and any other suffering that we have experienced in our lives because we have supposedly sinned: when we did something we were not supposed to do, something labeled bad, and got in trouble with others or especially with ourselves. Then he guides us to again fully suffer for these bad things that we recall in this present moment. He also instructs us to turn this

---

21 Manly P. Hall: *The Secret Teachings of All Ages* Jeremy P. Thacher/Penguin, . New York, NY: p. 119. (First printed, 1936),

around by giving thanks for this event, by giving thanks for this lesson of the consequences of this self-judgment, and by giving thanks for this opportunity to experience compassion for ourselves in our remembered adventures of supposed badness. My head is shaking. I think, "This is not what I was originally taught; this actually sounds like the opposite of what I was taught." But soon, I give myself permission to try this out. "Anything experienced fully turns to joy," he reminds us. So I jump into suffering again for specific past sins that now come to mind. I fully allow myself to be in the hell of self-judging and the shame that I've known so well. Then suddenly I laugh at myself. I hear other people; first they may have been moaning and crying, and now, like me, they too are laughing. Soon most of us are laughing at our ridiculous behaviors, our so-called sins.

By the end of the day we spontaneously make up a song: "We are the bad ones, and we love ourselves." This song has many spontaneously composed verses, I'm noticing with delight. Soon we are all dancing and singing this song. I notice that I feel the most self-love that I've ever known.

—Buck in India

The idea of oneness was not missed by many of the world's great spiritual teachers. Nanak, the first Sikh guru, taught in India around 1500 CE, when there was great strife between Hindus and Muslims. He pointed out the idea of oneness when he said: "There are no Muslims; there are no Hindus."

When Jesus tells his disciples that they will do even greater works than he has done, he is implying that they, like him, are one with

God. The Gospel of Thomas, which is not included in the Bible, takes the idea of oneness much further. It quotes Jesus as saying,

> *"When you make the two into one, and when you make the inner like the outer, the outer like the inner, and the upper like the lower, and when you make male and female into a single one, so that the male will not be male nor the female be female, when you make an eye in place of eyes, a hand in place of hands, a foot in place of feet, an image in place of images, then you will enter [the kingdom]."*

—*Jesus*

To summarize, the three basic ideas that underlie this method are:

1. Belief is a block.
2. Trust your own experiences.
3. Avoid dualism.

These core principles came to us in hindsight after we re-explored the Christian Bible. If you give yourselves this type of experience, you can expect that you will get additional and personally powerful insights and unique understanding. Sacred literature can thereby become a personal adventure, an exploration of self. We discovered that we could understand our own personal histories in much greater depth. Our newfound insights into ourselves have amazed us. We expect that you too will be delighted to take this inner journey and to gain valuable insights from doing so.

> *Know yourself.*
> *Understand yourself.*
> *Forgive yourself.*
> *Forget yourself.*

—*Isan, Zen Master*

Can Christians be Saved?

Isan's teaching is very simple: we can get to enlightenment only after we truly understand ourselves and have forgiven and forgotten ourselves. Before this and the major part of the journey, however, comes learning and understanding who we really are. This book deals with these first two steps. A big part of this process is sorting out our true self from a huge and often deeply hidden amount of subconscious programming that has come from our families, our culture, and particularly religious dogma. We hope to reveal how to use sacred teachings for self-deprogramming and self-understanding. Thus we prepare for the final steps of our journey to our true self.

Who Am I?

I am Oneness
And the end of Duality.
I am existence, consciousness, bliss

The Eastern contemplative traditions have developed ways of knowing the world directly through the textbook of immediate experience[22].

—Gitanand

Experience becomes our teacher. By the use of these methods, Biblical allegories, not dogma, become the source of the truth that can guide us. We can feel freedom from our old programming and the dogmatic religious beliefs that have been instilled in us, directly or indirectly. In this series of experiences, we found change. The Christianity that we had mostly abandoned became revitalized. The impact of these experiences has been greatly enhanced by our simultaneous study of oneness.

✲✲

22 Quoted by Cope Stephen: *Yoga and the Quest for the True Self* (New York, NY: Bantam, 2000), p. 71.

Chapter 3

Old Testament Allegories

Introduction: Experiencing the Bible as Allegories

This chapter is about the Old Testament. We started with Jesus. But inconsistencies drove us back to the Old Testament. This is why.

As I ride the donkey colt into Jerusalem, just as the prophet predicted, I hear the people shouting: "This is Jesus, the prophet from Nazareth of Galilee." But what do I feel? One moment I am clear as to what I'm doing, as when I healed the two blind men who were sitting by the road back a ways. But in the very next moment, a great anger seems to stir in me, and as I go into the great temple of my Father, this anger boils over. I observe myself charging through the courtyard, whip in hand, driving out the merchants and turning over the tables of the money changers and shouting out: " It is written, 'My house shall be called a house of prayer,' but you have made it a den of thieves." I feel such a powerful alignment with the wrath of my Father, Jehovah, and the anger of disappointment often expressed by the prophets of old.

After this maddening day, a day of celebration, healing, and warring, I feel so conflicted that I have to get away from it all, so I escape alone to Bethany to try to recollect myself. However, as I waken to begin my new day and to return to the city, I am extremely hungry. I spot a fig tree, and in great expectation, I go up to it, but it has no figs. My anger explodes again, and I shout out: "Let no fruit grow on you ever again." I immediately kill that loathsome tree, which failed to respect my need and my status as the Son of Jehovah.[23]

—Buck as Biblical Jesus

The puzzle that we couldn't deal with was that Jesus kept speaking with two voices. When talking, he would frequently switch from being judgmental to being loving. Sometimes he would speak as the Old Testament God of Judgment and Punishment, and sometimes as the New Testament God of Love. For example, Jesus spoke judgmentally when he got angry at the fig tree when it didn't have any figs for him and his disciples when they were hungry. So he killed the tree![24] He spoke about loving when he said to love our enemies. The confusion from reading the words of Jesus led us to go back to the starting point of Christian teaching, the allegory of the Garden of Eden at the beginning of Genesis. With our investigation of the Creation story, we began to see the parallelism between the two voices of Jesus and the two trees in the center of the garden. All of a sudden, we understood the symbolism of these two trees. The

---

23 Based on Matthew 21
24 Matthew 21:19.

tree of life symbolizes oneness,[25] while the tree of the knowledge of good and evil symbolizes duality. Then we supposed that it took the three years of the ministry of Jesus for him to make the full transition between these two competing ideas about God.

When this productive insight came to us from this first Old Testament allegory, then it seemed obvious that we needed to experience other foundational allegories from this book before we could really understand the New Testament. And as we continued our work, we became more convinced that this is true, at least for us.

Our general approach is to give a brief summary of the story of each specific allegory that we examined and then report on our experiences as we relive the story. Often we include our back and forth discussion as each of our individual experiences as these would stimulate further insights to the other. At the end, we provide a summary of the lesson provided to us by our combined experiences.

Caution:

The lessons that you get from experiencing these allegories should provide you with your own personal truths and might be quite different from what we learned. This is OK; in fact, it is the intention of this work with sacred allegories. This indeed is the value of experienced based learning because it provides us with our own personal truths.

The Garden of Eden

The Original Story: *God planted a garden eastward of Eden, and there He put the man whom He had formed. God made every tree grow that is pleasing to the sight and good for food. The tree of life was also in*

---

25 Oneness is unity thinking, in contrast to dualistic thinking, and is described in more detail in the Introduction on page 6.

the midst of the garden and the tree of the knowledge of good and evil. God commanded the man, saying, "Of every tree of the garden you may freely eat. But of the tree of the knowledge of good and evil, you shall not eat, for the day that you eat of it, you shall surely die." God made Eve, a woman, from one of Adam's ribs. They were both naked, the man and his wife, and were not ashamed. The serpent then appears to Eve and convinces her to eat the fruit of the tree of the knowledge of good and evil. She shares this with Adam. Then the eyes of both were opened, and they knew that they were naked, and they sewed fig leaves together and made themselves coverings. God, finding out what they had done, threw them out of the Garden of Eden so that they couldn't eat from the tree of life and live forever.[26]

God

The Biblical story was told from the perspective of Adam and Eve, as they told the story to their children. From my perspective, it is a little different.

Before they ate the fruit from the tree, we were in paradise together, and there was no separation between them and me. We were as one, enjoying not only the beauty, but also the stillness and infinity of the garden. There was no judgment, no separation, and I never warned them about the tree of the knowledge of good and evil because they understood very clearly that eating its fruit was a poor choice. Eating of the fruit of that tree is like choosing to live in a shack when the finest penthouse in the world is available. It is so far below the existence of the garden that

---

26 Taken from Genesis 1&2.

eating of it was repulsive. Nevertheless, they were tricked into doing exactly that.

I was shocked when I saw how their thoughts and behavior had been changed and modified by the tree of duality. They judged themselves to be naked, they judged themselves to be wrong and ashamed, and, worst of all, they judged me now to be angry, judgmental, mean, and unforgiving. The Fall of Adam and Eve was in their eyes also my Fall.

What was I to do? I tried to tell them that it was OK and to come back to being one with me, but they could not hear me. It was as if they now saw me and heard me through a curtain. When I would say something to them, it would register with them differently. Instead of seeing me as loving, they saw me as angry. The fruit of that tree had changed them so that they did not know me. The story says that I threw them out of the garden, when actually they left in their shame on their own. How sad I was that day. How lonely I felt.

After they left, I sat in the garden and pondered all that had transpired. How could I get them to come back? How could I change their new dualistic way of thinking? I could not undo what they had done, but I could form a plan whereby their descendants could discover a way back to the garden. I knew that if I told them how to get back, they would not hear it the way I said it because of the curtain that was in front of them and all around them. Perhaps I could hide the secrets somehow for them to discover through their investigation and experience the way back. Yes, that is it! Now I feel the old hope returning that there is a way to do this. One day, we will all be together again. And the beauty of it all is that a thousand years will seem like a day to me.

—Virginia as God

Virginia Speaks

The reader will notice that this view of God is a departure from the literal view of God in the Old Testament. Since the writers of the Bible operated from a Dualistic mindset, God in Genesis was seen as the God of Dualism, and was seen as vindictive, angry and judgmental, as well as the creator and nurturer. As I read the story of the garden, I chose to see the God of the garden as non-dualistic (Oneness), with a heart of compassion for Adam and Eve. I also see that Adam and Eve helped to create the dualistic God by their reaction to falling into duality. And they assumed that God was also like them, feeling separation. It is important, I think, that the non-dualistic God was also planning the way back to the garden for Adam and Eve. In the literal interpretation, if we see the Bible from Genesis to Revelation, the Dualistic God was also planning this. I love it when we see that spiritual threads come full circle. But the difference is that with the Dualistic God, the divine is "out there", while in the Oneness plan, God resides internally in us all.

The Devil

Before I tell you the story of Adam and Eve, let me explain myself. God and I have been twins since forever. God is the artist, the creative one; I am the jokester and the destroyer. So once upon a time, God got into a really big creative mode and worked for six days straight to create a universe. I mean he created everything imaginable.

40

And the crowning jewel of His creation was the Garden of Eden with His two loveable inhabitants, Adam and Eve. Now me, I just had to go there and see what mischief I could stir up. In the center of His garden, God planted two trees. At first, they were puny trees. So I sneaked into His garden and cut the top off of one of His trees. This one grew in the shape of a Y, while the other one grew straight and tall.

Today, the day of the story, I go into the garden, intending to play a joke on Adam and Eve. I see the tree that I had topped. It, like the other tree, has matured, and now it is with fruit, beautiful fruit. I remember that God told Adam and Eve not to eat of this tree. He didn't tell them His reason, but I'll tell you now. He didn't want them to know what He knows; He wants to keep them as His toys and under His control. Well, let's just see about that.

I turn myself into a serpent so that I can slither up the tree and pick its most beautiful fruit and bring it down to Eve. I know that she is hungry. I give her the fruit, explaining to her how delicious it is. Adam walks up just now, and Eve shows him the fruit. He too is hungry, and they also feel sexy. Eve puts her lips to one side of the fruit and motions for Adam to do the same. They both bite lustily into the fruit and chew it while starring seductively into each other's eyes. As I watch, I see their expressions change. They back away from each other, remembering that God had warned them not to eat the fruit of this tree. I enjoy my success as I see their expressions turn to horror. They look at each other's naked bodies and realize, as if for the first time, that anatomically, they are not the same. They blush, run, and hide under the fig tree. God is coming and is calling to them. Quickly, they grab some fig leaves and cover up their most obviously different body parts.

Reluctantly, they come out from under the tree and sheepishly appear before God. Both are feeling guilty and embarrassed because He originally told them that they would die if they ate the fruit of the tree of the knowledge of good and evil. Well, He couldn't just strike them dead, so he throws open the gate for them, and they run out of the garden in shame. They find themselves in the open world, where they will have to struggle to eke out a living. But God's disappointment is not limited to Adam and Eve; He also is furious with me. And He says to me with great anger: "You snake, you, forevermore, you'll retain this body form, and you will have to twist about on your belly in the dust."

Well, my revenge is making a curse that the dualistic thinking generated by partaking of the fruit of the tree of the knowledge of good and evil will also last many generations. Therefore, so long as humans continue to view their world dualistically, they will fear God rather than love Him as He intended.

—Buck as the Devil

Buck Speaks

To the dualistic mind, there is a need for the opposite of God. And as God was the one who created things, the opposite was the one who set out to destroy things. This character, not recognized as a god, in traditional Christianity, yet having godlike powers was called the Devil. In this case he is the bad actor.

Eve

Adam, God, and I are together in the garden. I am happy and enjoy our lives together and the great beauty of this place. I am beautiful. Every part of me sparkles.

One day, I'm alone, and the serpent appears, holding this delicious piece of fruit. He hands it to me. I feel a bit uneasy and sense that this fruit is different from all the other fruit in the garden. I notice that this is the first time that I've ever questioned anything that the garden has provided for us. Also, I feel hungry and want to eat. Adam walks up and sees me with some food. Without thinking, I share with Adam, as we always do. After tasting the bite of fruit, I am startled. My sparkles are disappearing. I have changed. Adam also appears different. We are naked! We are hiding from God and covering ourselves with fig leaves. But why are we hiding from God? And why are we covering ourselves? We've never even thought of doing this before. God asks us why we ate the fruit of the tree of the knowledge of good and evil. Adam blames me; I blame the serpent. God throws us out of the garden.

Oh, this is Adam's fault. I don't feel close anymore—not to Adam, not to God. I'm in a desperate place! And I've lost all of my sparkles. I wonder whether God will ever let us back into the garden. I had such wonderful feelings of oneness there in the garden.

—Virginia as Eve

Buck Speaks

When separate from God, and unable to receive God's grace we loose the light that results from the presence of the divine within. Our shine or sparkle is gone along with our joy. We often feel like the victim and we are ashamed of ourselves.

Adam

I smell such wonderful fragrances and love looking at all these surroundings. Wow! Everything is pleasant. I love what I see, smell, touch, hear, and taste. I sing, dance, and delight in the presence of Eve. She has a beautiful smile and is really enjoying eating something. She hands it to me, and I take a bite. Delicious! But now there is this strange feeling. It's churning; words, ideas, and feelings rise from inside me. This has never happened before! I can talk and tell these things to Eve. She can do this too. But some of our feelings don't feel good. I look at Eve, but she doesn't look like me. She is different! I don't like this difference. I look down at myself and see that between my legs, I'm not like her! I feel separate from her. I really don't like this. I feel all mixed up in my head. Now I remember that she was over there with the serpent. She picked a fruit from that tree. Now I remember that this is the tree whose fruit God told us not to eat. I realize that this bite of fruit did something to us. I want to hide. My face feels red and hot. So does Eve's. Now I feel angry with her and the serpent. They made me do something that God told me not to do.

God comes into the garden. We run away to the fig tree and grab some leaves and cover ourselves up where we look different from each other. God is angry. I try to explain what has happened, but this just seems to make things worse, and God gets even angrier. Then He tells us about things that will happen to us because we disobeyed Him. I don't want these things to happen. Then He throws us out of the garden, and I feel really unhappy. I never had such feelings before.

This new place is bad; the garden was good. Now I know that things are either good or bad. Eve is bad; she gave me to eat that which I was not supposed to eat. The serpent is bad; he told Eve to eat the fruit of that tree. And God is bad, but I better not think that because if He finds out, he'll punish me with more bad things. Oh, so that's why the tree is called the tree of the knowledge of good and evil. I sure would like to eat of the other tree, the tree of life, but bad God (*Ekes! I better not think that*) won't let me back into the garden. God does not want to let me get any more of its fruit.

—Buck as Adam

Buck Speaks

First man/first woman, Adam and Eve, in this allegory symbolize to me that period in evolution when the viewpoint of duality

45

and separateness began to be experienced and when humans became self conscious. The ego began forming. This likely happened slowly over a long period of time. This allegory makes it seemed to have happened at a single point in time. Thus to fully appreciate the meaning of this lesson, it was necessary for me assume otherwise.

Along with this step in human consciousness evolution, another human activity was developing in parallel. Concepts of God begin to develop in human thought, especially in certain places where civilizations were budding. The concept symbolized in this story is that of a God separate from us, something greater than us, and something with power over us. This separate being made us seem smaller and weaker by comparison. Notice how the ego became apparent when God returned to the garden and Adam and Eve were noticing their behavior and judging themselves as having done something wrong. It was their thinking and their concepts that caused them to believe that God was the cause their troubles.

A desire to gain some sort of control over this God led us humans to began devising religions – ideas and behaviors that we could employ to gain some powers by which we gain control over and benefit from this superior being. Also the idea of heaven was germinated during these times too; perhaps as a genetic memory of past times before the birth feelings of separateness came to us. Somehow we got the idea that Heaven was the property of God and only with God's permission could we ever get there. We thought God's requirements were stringent and extremely difficult to meet. And we were led to believe that only by these religions could we ever get our ancient desire to return to heaven fulfilled.

Obviously I'm reading more into Adam's experience than he ever realized. But steps in the evolution of human consciousness have taken long periods of time. Currently, many spiritual leaders such as Bhagavan envision that the next step in this evolutionary chain of events is taking place now as human conscious is beginning to shift from dualistic to non-dualistic thinking.

Two Trees

Two trees stood in a garden,
But these trees were much more than they first appeared,
For they symbolized two very different ideas about God.
One tree was called the tree of life,
The other the tree of the knowledge of good and evil.

Abraham chose the second tree
Because he worshiped the God of Fear,
> *The God of Judgment,*
> *A God who demands sacrifices*
> *And whose brother is the Devil.*

In a faraway place across the vast ocean
Hiawatha chose the first tree
Because he worshiped the God of Love
> *The God of Nonjudgment,*
> *A God of Peace and Compassion,*
> *And this god had no brother.*

Abraham's tribes fought wars,
Slew their enemies and their enemies' children,
And burned their houses.

Hiawatha's tribes made peace accords
And buried their implements of war in a hole left
When the tree of the knowledge of good and evil
Was toppled by all the people.
And there they planted a new tree, which grew magnificently,
Becoming known as the great tree of peace.

Can Christians be Saved?

Adam and Eve and the Devil

Now just who was that serpent in the Garden of Eden?
I say it was the voice of the inner judge.
And when listened to and obeyed, it becomes a god:
The God of Judgment,
The God of Shame, Punishment, Unforgiveness, and Suffering.
After eating the fruit of this God, Adam and Eve could no longer
Partake of the fruit of the tree of life. So they died.
But first Adam's punishment:
930 years of toil in the fields of thorns
And one of his sons murdered by the other son.
So the sins of guilt, blaming someone else,
Jealousy, and murder were born.
And behold!
They even had to cover their second chakras[27] with fig leaves!

A couple thousand years later, Jesus came, saying:
"God is Love, Forgiveness, and Compassion!"
"But wait, wait!" cried the Pharisees.
"We owe thousands of years of allegiance to the God of Judgment, and we'll
*   have it no other way!"*
For they excelled in judging, blaming, and expressing jealousy.
So they conned the Romans into killing the God of Love and then wrote a
*   Bible in which the words of the God of Judgment were often inserted*
*   in the mouth of Jesus.*
And the Romans were pleased and elected Jesus as the Son of God.
And humans still aren't allowed to approach the tree of life.

---

27 Chakras are energy centers in the body; the second chakra is in the region of the genitals.

God's Brother

Hey! Did you know that God's brother was a serpent,
That is, the God of the Old Testament.
Whoa! He talked a woman into thinking for herself,
And this made God so mad that he turned his brother into a snake
And made him crawl on the ground and eat dust.
It was many generations before women got brave enough
*   to think for themselves again.*

On the other side of the world,
Where no one knew the story of God's brother,
Women thought for themselves from the beginning
And they even got the right to vote before men did![28]

Buck Discusses His Realizations

Two trees are described in perhaps the oldest of Jewish stories, the Creation story, which is set in the Garden of Eden. Each tree symbolizes a different idea about God. The tree of life provides humans with the idea that God is a single force, the law of love. This is oneness. The tree of the knowledge of good and evil provides the alternative idea that God is dualistic—one side, God, is good, while the other side, the Devil, is evil.[29] When Adam and Eve ate the fruit from the tree of the knowledge of good and evil, it showed humans, collectively, as taking in the idea or concept that there were two forces operating in both our individual and collective minds. President Obama, in his recent Nobel Prize acceptance speech, expressed this dualistic concept in our present-day thinking: *"Adhering to this law*

---

28 In the Iroquois Confederacy, which provided about 900 years of peace amongst the Northeastern tribes of North America, only the women had the right to vote.

29 It was Philo of Alexander, in late pre-Christian Egypt, who first pointed out that these trees are symbolic.

of love has always been the core struggle of human nature. We are fallible. We make mistakes and fall victim to the temptations of pride, power, and sometimes evil." His statement indicates that we collectively still believe in evil.

Prior to eating the fruit, Adam and Eve were naked and innocent, happy and carefree; after eating, they hid their nudity, feeling guilty and ashamed. They were afraid of God. For the first time, they felt separate from each other and separate from God. Oneness had ended; the tree of life was almost forgotten. Duality was established. Judgment and punishment were in the minds of humans and became a basic premise of the evolving Western religions.

In contemplating the story of the Garden of Eden, the thing that stood out was that they ate the fruit of the wrong tree! Suddenly, they had internalized the idea that the world was divided into good and evil. From the studies of other religions, including some of those of the Native Americans, it becomes obvious that not everybody has eaten from the same tree. But those who had taken in this fruit of this second tree started judging themselves and each other, and their descendants continued to do so; all of them were ashamed, and they started feeling separate from each other and separate from God. Judging on the scale of good and evil is the way our culture teaches us to think. Most of us have thought this way all of our lives; people have done so throughout recorded history. Yet we also knew, at least intellectually, that it was also possible to think another way—the way symbolized by the tree of life. One wrong bite, and a large part of humankind was off into a misery-making way of thinking. This realization led us to read the Rev. Deborah L. Johnson's book *Your Deepest Intent*. In that book, Johnson explains this allegory of Creation in a very similar way. Her writings helped us to understand our realization even more deeply. This wasn't something that we had thought up on our own. The idea of these two differing view of God is as old as time itself, but it had been a secret to us.

What a clever story! What a great allegory! And we have been misled all of our lives by the fundamentalist Christian teaching that this is really history. Not that we could really believe that this was history, but we just never stopped to think, until now, what this story was trying to teach us.

50

Another realization from our revisiting of the Garden of Eden allegory was the impact of this story on the way in which women have been treated. This story has been used to rationalize discrimination against women.

Also, we've been told repeatedly and are still told today that Christianity, Judaism and Islam are monotheistic. Both God and the Devil are introduced in this story. How can this be monotheism?

Virginia Speaks

In the story of the Garden of Eden, Adam and Eve believe the serpent, instead of remembering the relationship that they had with God and trusting God instead of the serpent. So God punishes them by banishing them from the garden. This to me is an allegory of the fracture of the spiritual parts of myself and the story of the parts coming back together during my life journey.

I always wanted to do some great thing for God, to be used by God to change my world. I thought that being a good Christian would provide a way for me to do this. I became a Christian minister for this reason and pastored churches in Florida and New Mexico. In my years in ministry, I helped many people, preached many sermons, and sang many songs of praise to Jesus. But the desire of my heart, my longing to be close to God, to be used by God, was actually my longing to love myself completely, to forgive myself, and then to be released from the bondage of otherness into experiencing life as the sum of my parts: whole, complete, and fully aware of the joy of being alive.

This song speaks of the beauty of the union with God (self):

> He speaks, and the sound of His voice
> Is so sweet that the birds hush their singing,
> And the melody that he gave to me
> Within my heart is ringing. . . .[30]

---

30 "In the Garden," Words and Music by C. Austin Miles, 1912.

Instead of hearing this song as a statement of walking with a third-person God, I saw it as a beautiful experience of the realization of God within. This process of returning to myself began when I left the ministry. The view of the Bible as infallible and literal had splintered my soul. I was looking at this life as a time of working hard so that I would deserve heaven after this life. I was seeing my life as one that demanded obedience to a set of rules, which I failed to honor sufficiently, which brought guilt, shame, and fear. I was looking outside myself for salvation, and the places told to me by Christianity that contained salvation were "out there"; they were not inside me.

I remembered that during the time I attended college, I practiced Zen Buddhism for three years. The practice of mindfulness has been with me since then. I like the quietness of a still mind, represented by a smooth lake surface: peacefulness and contentment. After rereading the story of Adam and Eve, I, like them, wanted to return to what they had lost: a garden unblemished. It was then that I realized that I have had this all along: a still mind, my garden within.

Conclusion from the Garden of Eden Experiences

In the Garden of Eden story, we see that the secrets hidden are foundational and timeless in realizing higher states of consciousness. We have a choice: remain mired in the judgment and separation of dualism, or find the spiritual pathways to the tree of life, oneness. It is interesting that the modern-day controversy of the story is whether Christians should believe in evolution or creation science. Compared with the question of duality, it is a great waste of time to argue evolution, fighting it out through the literalism of the scriptures. The universal pivotal question of our day is whether we can evolve spiritually into oneness to save our planet and its inhabitants. This choice, hidden in Genesis, has been put to us since the beginning.

Abraham

The Original Story*: Now it came to pass that God tested Abraham, saying "Take your only son Isaac to the land of Moriah, and offer him as a burnt offering." The next morning, after Abraham packed up what he needed, he, Isaac, two young men helpers, and a donkey left for the mountain. He took Isaac and the supplies up the mountain, leaving the two men and the donkey at base camp. Isaac questioned his father for not having a lamb to sacrifice, to which Abraham replied: "My son, God will provide for Himself the lamb for the burnt offering." After building the altar and placing the firewood, Abraham bound Isaac and placed him on the altar. When Abraham stretched out his hand and took the knife to slay his son, an angel stopped Abraham and provided a ram to be used instead. Then, because Abraham was willing to follow God's command, God spoke and said: "I will bless you, and I will multiply your descendants as the stars of the heavens and as the sand that is on the seashores, and your descendants shall possess the gate of their enemies. In your seed, all the nations of the earth shall be blessed, because you have obeyed my voice."[31]*

It is a wonderful day, and I enjoy my life with my growing son Isaac. I teach him things that I've learned in my long life. God appears and tells me to prepare to make a sacrifice to Him on a distant mountain. The sacrifice is to be Isaac! I am aghast, but I hide my feelings from God. I examine myself and realize that there is a part of me who is very like Jehovah and is often completely adamant about my ideas. It is a very masculine part, a part that is completely stiff-necked and won't take no for an answer. So I give into God's request, knowing that there is no way He would

---

31 Genesis 22:1–18

be willing to change His mind. I see no point in challenging the great God Jehovah. After all, He did give me this son when my wife and I were too old to have children. Still, I am angry, but I seem to be succeeding in hiding my anger from God. I give every appearance of obeying, and I do exactly as I am told. On the mountaintop, I experience great agony as I raise the knife to plunge it into the heart of my beloved and only son. I feel surprised that God doesn't notice that my obedience is not completely honest. I also realize that I am training my son to obey me, just as I obey God. I feel deeply for Isaac and am amazed that his behavior is so like mine. I start to plunge the dagger into Isaac's heart, but an angel of God stops me. He points to a ram caught in a bush that I am to use as the sacrifice instead of my son. I feel relief, but my anger at God does not dissipate.

The sacrificial ceremony ends. God is pleased and rewards me for my obedience as He tells me: "I will bless you, and I will multiply your descendants as the stars of the heavens and as the sand on the seashores, and your descendants shall possess the gate of their enemies." Instantly, I realize how I'll get revenge for this painful act of God's.

We go back down the mountain, and my plan is realized. I set the intention deep into my genetic code. The intention is that among my many descendants, at least one will rebel and change gods. At this time, I don't know that this will take a couple of thousands of years and that the rebel descendant will be called Jesus.

I leave the mountain and go to Beersheba, where I start the process of having more children to take advantage of God's promise and make sure that the seed of my deeply held intent will survive.

—Buck as Abraham

Buck has Further Insights

Who is my internal Abraham? Who is my internal Isaac? Who is this God-self who demands obedience and sacrifice? And who is my goat with its head caught in the bush? These are the many forms of my denial!

Abraham is the part of me that was willing to sacrifice my inner boy. My father could become very angry and therefore dangerous. So I learned to obey, really carefully obey. What he expected me to sacrifice was my sissiness. The goat that became the substitution for the sacrifice was my denial of the truth. I had lived well into adulthood before I was willing to do anything rather than tell myself or others that I was gay. Yes, I was an Isaac simply doing what my father-god expected me to do, even if I died in the process.

The Angel

As an angelic being and herald, I see a great many events and lives upon the earth. All of those lives are very precious to me as they are the Creation of the Divine. There was much spiritual energy around Abraham, and I was drawn in the spirit to watch out for him. He really wanted to serve God, but since the Fall from the garden, he was like all the rest of the people. God had become something "out there," separate from them, and understanding a god like that can be difficult. So I picked him up one day as he was carrying Isaac up the mountain, and I followed his steps. When he reached the summit, I realized that he meant to kill his son as a sign to God that God could trust Abraham. My heart was overcome with emotion and compassion for Abraham because he so wanted to love God and do some great thing for God, but Abraham had misunderstood how to do that. Rebuking him for that was the last thing that I wanted to do, but I had to prevent him from killing his son. So I ran down the mountain until I found an animal that he could substitute for his son and flew back up to the summit, where Abraham was raising the knife to kill his son. I appeared to Abraham and gently told him that God had heard his prayer and that God provided a substitute for his son. Abraham was so relieved that he began to weep and thank me. He then released Isaac. Isaac also was relieved, but they were both scared. I then blessed them both, but especially did I bless Abraham with wisdom for future spiritual decisions. As I did these things, I felt as though I had done a part to keep humanity headed back to the garden, to a place before the Fall.

—Virginia as the Angel

Virginia Comments

I offer an alternative view of the story. Instead of assuming that God told Abraham to kill his son to prove his faith, suppose we consider that this experience was a result of Abraham's desire to do a great thing for God and to prove his worthiness to God. Abraham mistakenly thought that killing Isaac would accomplish that. I know that I had a time in my life when I wanted to serve God, but I made an unwise decision about how to do it.

I was in my twenties and believed that the Bible was literally true. I wanted to be used by God and to serve Him. I had become a minister at a nondenominational church in Florida. I heard of a church called Maranatha in Gainesville, Florida. Maranatha was a radical group of young Christians who were overseen by a group of elders who made the decisions for all of the members. Maranatha's goal was to win the world for Christ by setting up churches on university campuses worldwide. After praying about it, my spouse and I decided to join, and we moved to Gainesville to join with Maranatha and be trained to go across the U.S. and then the world to preach the gospel of God. In just a year or so, we were sent out with another couple to begin a ministry at the University of New Mexico in Albuquerque. We moved all of our belongings from Florida to New Mexico, rented an old fraternity house, and began to preach to the students and move those students who believed into the frat house.

We became increasingly disenchanted with the ministry because of the pressure put upon us as local ministers by the elders to control the lives of the students and force them to behave in "good Christian" ways. The women in the church were expected not to weigh over a certain amount. All members were to dress a certain way and to be at all the meetings or face church discipline. Well, early on, I decided that all this was ridiculous, so I stopped applying these rules or dogma in my local church. However, every so often, some of the elders would visit and criticize and threaten me because my church was unruly and undisciplined.

The final straw came when the elders announced in the early 1980s that AIDS was God's punishment on gays. I immediately thought that this was preposterous, as the God who I thought had sent his Son to die for all would never send an Old Testament plague to kill a certain group of people. My spouse and I decided to leave the church.

As a result of this experience, I knew that we had made a mistake to join Maranatha, even though we helped many people, made many friends, and relocated to a wonderful city.

Similarly, I believe that Abraham was well-meaning, but misunderstood how to have faith in his God. As I channeled the angel, I recognized that the angel did not judge Abraham or get angry with Abraham because he had mistakenly decided to kill Isaac. The angel was moved with compassion and provided a way for Abraham to see a substitution for Isaac so that Abraham would not do so dreadful a thing as to kill his son. The angel saved two lives that day: not only Isaac's, of course, but also Abraham's life too. If Abraham had killed his son, Abraham would have been filled with guilt for all time.

We can learn to forgive ourselves when we make poor decisions in life. We can have compassion for ourselves and go on in life, having learned a valuable lesson and with the expectation to make better decisions in the future. Because of this self-compassion, we can also learn to forgive those who hurt us rather than to let our egos allow us to feel justifiable anger towards or judgment of others. Also, as we have compassion, we can do the work of the angel and save others from making a mistake that they will regret.

Virginia Continues

As I sat with the story of Abraham and Isaac, I remembered the story of Virginia and Elizabeth.

For many years, I carried the death of my daughter as a burden of pain and sorrow. Elizabeth, who was born almost thirty years ago, was born with anencephaly. She lived only seven days, but my spouse, Lee, and I loved her for those seven days. We were told in Lee's third month of pregnancy that Elizabeth had this condition, and an abortion was advised. At that time, we did not believe in abortion, being fundamentalist Christians. We agreed that we would pray for the child's healing. Lee was one of the most courageous people I have ever known.

We prayed for the healing every day until our child was born, but we also prayed and told her that we loved her and that we would welcome her at birth. And we did. She was a precious gift, if only for seven days.

After her death, I went through the motions of forgiving God or hating the Devil for the loss, but I tried to appreciate her short life more than my individual grief. Many years later, as I was discovering myself and my unity with the Universe, I revisited my feelings about Elizabeth's life and death. Through sorrow, grief, and the deep pain of the experience, I had my own challenge finally to bond with my daughter after many years, rather than viewing her death as a time of failure, sorrow, and pain. My pain was so real even after many years that I cried and cried and almost gave up. But just as the angel showed Abraham the goat to substitute for Isaac, so I found new eyes, hope and love, to replace my sorrow and pain. I forgave the God who was there in my life at the time, as I forgave myself in the present for my misunderstanding, bitterness, and rage at the event. As Elizabeth and I walked down from the mountain together, I knew that we both were healed.

Buck Reports on Becoming Isaac

A month or so after experiencing Abraham, I got to experience Isaac, not on purpose, but as a result of a spontaneous situation. I was working with a friend who had a dream. The friend's dream was of seeing a young boy walking home, apparently in fear. My friend approaches the boy and asks whether he wants some help. The boy backs away in fear. This is the sum total of the dream.

So after getting my friend to retell the dream in the present tense, I asked him to tell the dream as the boy while standing up and going through the movements while recounting the dream. While doing this, my friend was unable to allow himself to feel the boy's fear. The boy says that he is afraid of the man offering help (my friend), but I really can't detect any feelings of fear in his expression or actions. I then stand up and take the position of the boy. I ask my friend to resume the position of himself. I, as the boy, speak to him, expressing my fears as the boy. I allow myself to feel the boy's fears fully. Our conversation turns to my asking him whether I can trust him. By this time, we both are becoming aware that the boy is his inner child. I, the boy, beg with teary eyes: "I want to trust you. I'll trust you if you promise not to commit suicide." I keep repeating this request, but the man just stands immobile, appearing to be deep in thought. Finally, he replies, "I can't make such a promise to you right now." By this time, we are both aware that if the man kills himself, he will also be killing me, his inner child. I certainly don't want this to happen, and I feel overwhelmed with this heavy feeling that I may be murdered by someone I'm trying to love. With these realizations, we conclude the process.

After this session, I felt utterly exhausted, probably because I was still carrying the unresolved heavy emotions of my friend's inner child. The next morning, still exhausted, I asked my friend Gurubhai, a powerful healer, to help me release this weariness.

Gurubhai begins massaging my chest. I am starting to feel what I felt at the end of the previous day's dream session. I ask permission to allow myself to fully express these emotions. Soon, I'm sobbing uncontrollably, and I continue this for several minutes until I believe that I've fully expressed these emotions. But Gurubhai reports that he is still detecting residual pain in my chest and presses on the spot where he notices this. When he does this, I instantly become Isaac tied down to the altar. My father, Abraham, is standing over me, knife aimed exactly at the spot in my chest where the tension remains. Now I fully experience Isaac's fear, sadness, and terror at expecting to be killed in an instant by my dearly beloved father. More wailing pours out of me. This continues for a little while until I suddenly remember Gurubhai doing a silly little dance, imitating his two-year-old grandson. I burst out laughing. So does Gurubhai. I am no longer carrying the pent-up emotions of my friend's inner child, nor the residual emotion from living through the Abraham story. And I fondly remember Bhagavan's teaching: "Anything when experienced fully becomes joy." This is an exercise I experienced in my oneness training, first in Fiji and then in India.

Conclusion

Through Abraham, we can see the result of the duality that he experienced in his life. He so wanted to please the God who was out there that he considered that killing Isaac could lead to getting closer to God. Delusions such as this one are common because we believe in good and evil through a dualism mindset. Therefore, we label people and even nations as evil. This way, we are justified in our violence or harmful actions against them. A modern example is the conservative church's war on gay, lesbian, bisexual, and transgender people. The church wants not only to brand these folk as wrong, but also to continue legal discrimination against them through limiting their rights as citizens.

Individually, we see these dualism delusions appearing in relationships when we feel that our partner or friend has done something to hurt us. Instead of finding forgiveness and love for them in oneness, we judge them as evil, our rationalization for yelling at them or cheating them as much as possible through the divorce process. We may even use such a judgment to justify inflicting physical harm on them. Another example is the business bottom line of profits becoming the only thing important to a company, causing its managers to forsake the care and security of the employees.

Oneness allows us to take the seeming crises of our lives and see us grow in our understanding of ourselves, as well as to experience healing for our pain and sorrow. Like Virginia and the healing of her relationship with her long-deceased daughter, we can find peace and love for ourselves and our world through oneness.

Joseph and His Coat of Many Colors

The Original Story. *Joseph was the youngest and the favorite son of Jacob. Joseph's father gave Joseph a tunic of many colors. He had dreams suggesting that his brothers would bow down to him. In jealousy, his* *brothers sold Joseph into slavery. As an Egyptian slave, Joseph became famous after interpreting one of Pharaoh's dreams. This dream, according to Joseph's interpretation, predicted seven years of abundance, followed by seven years of famine. Joseph was appointed to deal with this problem and became very powerful. When his brothers came to Egypt for supplies, he helped them, although they did not recognize who Joseph was. Eventually, Joseph was reunited with his parents.[32]*

Additional Analysis of the Story by Virginia

The story of Joseph[33] is one of the longest stories in the Bible. It chronicles the life of Joseph from his birth to his death and is an example of a story of death and rebirth. Joseph is almost killed by his brothers, who hate him and who sell him into slavery. Joseph is carried far away and experienced rebirth in his rise as one of the most powerful persons in the world.

Joseph is sold to Potiphar, a wealthy Egyptian officer of Pharaoh. Joseph is recognized for his intrinsic merit as an excellent administrator and is promoted to have charge over all lands of his master. But Potiphar's wife unjustly accuses Joseph of attempted rape, and he is put into prison, where again, because of his talents, he is made an overseer. He becomes known as an accurate interpreter of dreams. One day, he is pulled from the Egyptian prisons to interpret Pharaoh's dreams and is rewarded with honor and power. After taking care of his brothers, he reveals himself to them, and he saves his family and the world from famine. Joseph experiences four rebirths.

Joseph endures much suffering, from being rejected by his brothers to being falsely accused of rape by Potiphar's wife. The miraculous part of the story is that Joseph kept being restored to favor and kept using his gifts for the sake of others. His story is a wonderful example of how we can find favor when we are in the moment. Joseph was a slave, yet he found favor with Potiphar. Joseph was in

---

32 Retold childhood from memory
33 Genesis 37–50

prison, yet found favor with his jailers. Joseph used his gift of dream interpretation and found favor with Pharaoh. Whatever his circumstances, Joseph found glory, or favor, and was recognized for his gifts and accomplishments.

The other thing that is consistent throughout the story is that Joseph used the gifts that he had been given by God. Imagine being called before the president of the United States and being asked to interpret his dream. Talk about pressure! But Joseph was willing to risk being wrong or to look stupid to fulfill the responsibility of his gift. He interpreted the dream, and events all came to pass as he had foreseen. How many of us have gifts and talents that we do not use because we are afraid to be wrong or to look silly to others?

The final event in the story is when his brothers come to Egypt for food. How easy it would have been for Joseph to get his revenge and kill all of his brothers in retribution for how they had treated him. Instead, Joseph blessed them, forgave them, and saved all of them, along with their families. By using his gifts, he saved the world from starvation.

This allegory helped us to return to the mindset of oneness!

Buck Speaks

When I imagine myself as Joseph, my first thought is the coat of many colors. This says to me that my mother subconsciously recognized that I was gay. She actually denied this all of her life, but this fact didn't detract from my having this deep desire to be accepted by my mother as I actually was, even though I also denied my gayness for about the first thirty years of my life. Later, I did have a coat of many colors, and I did feel proud to identify with Joseph. I wore the coat until it was in tatters.

Joseph is still my hero! He endured many hardships, yet he succeeded when the odds against him were great. I was Joseph when I entered grade school. I was the only Anglo boy in my class; all the other students were children of Mexicans who had been made into American citizens against their will. This was a result of the

Can Christians be Saved?

Gadsden Purchase, which was signed in a little Mexican village, La Union, just five miles from where I was born. These people did not like Americans, especially white Americans, because these Mexican-Americans felt that they had been sold out to a foreign country, the United States of America. The children of these people acted out this hatred. The other boys in the school told one little boy whom I liked and who wanted to play with me that if he played with me, they would beat him up. Thus I shared an experience that was similar to Joseph's when his brothers, acting out of their jealousy, rejected him. I survived this experience and many other rejections throughout my life and somehow came bouncing back each time. Now I realize that it was Joseph who has been my subconscious role model. It was the image of him in his coat that gave me the incentive to keep on going with my life.

Virginia Speaks

Whenever I read the story of Joseph, I marvel again at the fact that he found favor with all those who came in contact with him, even if securing their favor took some time. This has also happened frequently in my life.

A good example was in 2003, when I was a lobbyist with the Coalition for Equality in New Mexico to pass laws that would protect and aid gay, lesbian, bisexual, and transgender (LGBT) people. During the sixty-day annual legislative session in 2003, I met and talked with most of the New Mexico legislators to educate them about LGBT issues and to answer any questions they might have about transgender issues. In the last week of the session, I got a call from another lobbyist. This caller said that Gov. Bill Richardson, who had supported our bills until then, might want to remove "gender identity" from the bill to make it easier to pass. The caller suggested that I ask for a meeting with the governor as soon as possible. I met the governor's aide, and he arranged for me to meet with the governor. At the appointed time, I met Gov. Richardson as his hairdresser and makeup artist prepared him for a TV appearance in the next hour.

After trading small talk, the governor asked me why I was there. I explained that I had heard that he planned to remove the protections for transgender people from the bill, and he said, "Virginia, I said that I would support trans-inclusion, and I will. I will do what I have pledged." Let me tell you, I walked out of his office feeling like Joseph coming from the audience with Pharaoh. Yes!

More Comments by Buck

Reading Virginia's analysis of Joseph's story challenged me to examine the deaths in my life. My first death was when I was about three years old. My father, who wanted to be a professional baseball player, decided that as he never had this chance in his life that he would give me the opportunity to do what he hadn't gotten to do. So he decided to start me playing ball at a very early age. About ten minutes or so into our first workout, he just couldn't get me to throw the ball the way in which he wanted me to throw it. He flew into a rage at the discovery that I would not be able to fulfill his dream and yelled at me, "You throw the ball like a girl, and you will never be able to play baseball. And I'll never play ball with you again!" Then he stomped off. Yes, I died at that moment, and even today, I cringe at the mere thought of picking up a ball. But it wasn't long until I picked up other hobbies—gardening and playing the piano—and found my happiness in these activities.

The next little death was when my first-grade friend told me he could not play with me anymore because the other boys would beat him up if he did so. I survived this by never getting out of view of the teacher who was monitoring the school yard during recesses.

The biggest death occurred when my wife insisted that we separate, and my little daughter grabbed me around my leg and begged me not to go. That night, my first night back in a dorm since my undergraduate days, I decided to kill myself. I took a razor blade and cut my wrists and wrapped a towel around my arm and went to sleep with my arm hanging over the side of the bed to let my blood drain out. I slept really soundly, perhaps because I was exhausted, given that I had hardly slept for the last month. I had been lying awake at night trying to solve a problem mentally that just wasn't mentally solvable. But in the early morning, I awoke; I wasn't dead. I was thirsty, agonizingly thirsty. Believing I had solved the unsolvable problem, I was finally able to sleep really well. Well-rested, I was rational for the first time in days.

I realized that I had to get a drink and that I could not raise my head above my heart, or I would faint. With my head lowered as far as possible, I got out of bed and got some water to drink. Then I called an ambulance and went to the emergency room just a block away. Soon a department head came to see me and asked what I wanted to do. He and the doctors in the emergency clinic recommended that I sign myself into the Phipps Clinic, the psychiatric clinic of the Johns Hopkins Hospital. I was a faculty member, so I had complete medical coverage. I went into the clinic believing that I had died to my old life and now was being given a totally new life with the chance to make it the life that would be right for me. During my last month in the hospital, I wrote my dissertation for my Ph.D. and graduated with my Ph.D. a few months later.

My last death was leaving the University of New Mexico as a consultant. I had been invited by the College of Pharmacy to help revive the Radiopharmacy teaching program. We established a consortium with the University of Arkansas and started teaching radiopharmacy over the Internet.

After helping to make this program highly successful, both academically and financially, I had a major problem with one of the staff members—one whom I originally hired to help get this program going. She started sabotaging what I was doing, and in this, she had the support of the other faculty member in this program and the dean of pharmacy. After months of this backstabbing, I could find no way to continue my teaching role in this program. The only alternative was to resign and retire. Instead of retiring completely, I immediately did a couple of landscaping projects, something I'd always wanted to do, but had never found the time to carry out. The transition into this new life was so quick and involving that I really didn't have time to look back at my previous life.

I conclude that each of my life's little deaths did provide an opportunity to resurrect myself and go on into a new dimension in life that I have really enjoyed.

Summary Comments by Virginia

As I made the story of Joseph the story of myself, I remembered the times of hardship from my life. Accept hardship and suffering in this life without value judgment, and move on to the next moment. If I dwell in the past, I will miss the blessing of the moment. During my gender transition from William to Virginia, these were the lessons that I learned:

1. When multiple hardships arise, reject the tendency to feel sorry for myself, and do not blame others. Move on to the NEXT blessing; do not get lost in the past.
2. Be quick to forgive, even for the most egregious wrongs done to me.
3. Expect favor and blessing to follow my life wherever I go.
4. Use my spiritual gifts. Never let fear cause me to hesitate using them.
5. Expect to encounter opportunities to bless others and to use my gifts. In the moment, these opportunities will be plentiful.
6. Show mercy and compassion to all, even when doing so is inconvenient.

This heart of compassion expressed toward his family enabled Joseph to save his family's world and for him to have power over the world in a benevolent sense. Showing mercy and compassion can change my world.

Conclusion

Through the story of Joseph, we can also see the two trees from the Garden of Eden in operation. Joseph represents the tree of life, while his brothers represent the tree of the knowledge of good and evil. His brothers were jealous and wanted to kill him. Eventually, they got rid of him. When they saw Joseph again, they were afraid that Joseph would kill them. Joseph, on the other hand, expected to be blessed wherever he was. He held no resentment toward his brothers. Joseph moved to save the world from famine.

A pathway to oneness is found in letting go of all harmful memories and emotions from our childhood, including our relationship with our parents, as well as all other primary relationships, and finding the ability and grace to love ourselves. Buck experienced this on one of his deaths, when he found new life after his suicide attempt. With that new hard-won meaning, he forgave himself and started fresh, clean, and whole. In all the crises in our lives, we can find new meaning if we resist the dualistic tendency to blame others for our problems. Oneness asks us to take responsibility for our actions and to create a better way as we learn to love ourselves and others.

Jonah and the Whale

Original Story: *God told Jonah to go to a city called Nineveh and to tell the people there that they were wicked and that their city was to be destroyed. Jonah did not want to do this, so he ran from God and hopped aboard a ship. A powerful storm arose, and all on the ship were afraid to die. The others on the ship thought that Jonah had caused the storm by disobeying God and threw him overboard to save themselves. Immediately, the storm abated, and a big fish swallowed Jonah. Jonah prayed, and the fish spit him out on dry land. Jonah then obeyed God, went to Nineveh, and warned the city. The people repented, and God did not destroy the city.*[34]

---

34 Summary of the Book of Jonah

Virginia Speaks

God is telling me to go and preach to the people of Nineveh and to tell them that He is going to destroy them if they don't repent. I feel fearful and inadequate. I just can't go to Nineveh, and I can't deliver this message to them; they will never listen to me. I also feel rebellious as I refuse God's challenge, yet I am afraid to disobey God, so I run away and take a boat that is leaving this place. A great storm arises, and the boat is about to capsize. The others on the boat know that I have disobeyed God and believe that this storm is God's way of punishing me. I feel their anger at me, which makes me fearful. I think that I should jump overboard, but I'm afraid to jump, even though I know that I'm at fault. The others on the ship are getting more afraid of the storm. I don't think that they want to kill me, but they want to save themselves, so they finally throw me overboard. A big fish immediately swallows me. I feel fear because I know that I am going to die in this fish's belly, yet, miraculously, I escape, so I decide to obey God. I go to Nineveh to preach of the death and destruction coming to Nineveh if its inhabitants don't repent. I am surprised; they all repent! Whew! I'm OK. They don't reject my preaching.

—Virginia as Jonah

Virginia Summarizes Her Experience and Insights

The story of Jonah and the whale (big fish) is a highly entertaining story. It provides a perfect example of our process. Using our

Gestalt technique, I became Jonah and experienced the story in the first person. What I saw was that if the Divine gives me a task or if I feel the grace to proceed, it does not matter what the obstacles or barriers might be. I just need to do it and know that the Divine will give me every tool and the wisdom needed to fulfill the task.

Several weeks before I wrote this, I attended a workshop on oneness. I was one of sixty attendees, yet I was the only transgender person at the meeting. At one of the morning breaks, a woman came up to me and wanted to talk. She said that she wanted me to know that being a woman is very hard. She expressed her resentment of "guys" who want to be women, as that encroaches upon women. She said that she thought that it is wrong for men to dress as women and to change themselves via surgery to be women. She thought that it was important for me to know where she stood on this. Well, here I am at a oneness conference! At what better time could this happen? Several years ago, I would have given her back several arguments as to why she was wrong. I would have told her that I am not a woman, but consider myself a two-spirit person, having elements and traits of both male and female. I would have told her about my past teachings and work on behalf of exposing the damage that patriarchy has had and is having on our culture. And I would have told her that many transgender persons, such as myself, experience a very literal stepping down from patriarchy when we transition to the other gender. So I would have done in the past, but on this occasion, I said none of these things, even though my ego desperately wanted me to say them. I did not do so because I felt such a compassionate heart for this woman.

I blessed her and thanked her for sharing her feelings and convictions with me. As she turned away and went back to her chair, I felt absolutely no defensiveness, anger, shame, or hurt. I simply felt challenged and thankful that she and I could practice oneness together, even though we disagreed about this issue. As I left the conference, I gave her my card and said that I would love to have coffee or lunch with her and talk further about all of this. She smiled at me, so who knows? We may yet have a time to come to understand each other.

The thing I saw was that God does give us the grace to love and to consider each other as one. Jonah did not feel that he could do what

God told him to do (to go to Nineveh and warn its inhabitants). Later, however, after all his trials, Jonah realized that God would give the power and grace for Jonah to be obedient. In a similar manner, I was given a wonderful opportunity to see that the Divine's grace empowers me to do anything that the Divine would have me do.

Buck Speaks

As I listened to Virginia as Jonah recounted his experience, what stood out for me was: Jonah's problem stayed the same. When God told Jonah to go to Nineveh, he expressed fear because he assumed that the people there would kill him. When he ran from God, Jonah expressed the same fear. He assumed that God would kill him. In the storm on the boat, Jonah expressed the same fear again: that the others on the boat would kill him. And still again, in the belly of the fish, he expressed fear that he would die inside the fish. Nonetheless, when God answered Jonah's prayer and the fish spit Jonah up upon the beach, he finally realized that he really had no other choice except to face his fear. And when he did, there was no problem. The people responded to his warning by fasting and changing their ways. Jonah was safe, the other people in the ship were safe, and the people of Nineveh were safe. Following the Divine seems to be worth doing.

Conclusion—Buck Speaks

This allegory says to me that when we have a deep-seated fear, I just can't run away from it because wherever I go or whatever I do, this fear is right here inside me. This lesson encourages me, and by example shows me that I must simply face the fear; I must do the fearful thing that I've been avoiding all along. And with divine grace, the problem caused by this fear will be solved.

✳✳

Chapter 4

New Testament Allegories

The Birth of Jesus

The Story: *To be registered in the census, Joseph traveled to Bethlehem with Mary, his betrothed wife, who was with child. She was a virgin. She brought forth her first-born son, wrapped him in swaddling clothes, and laid Him in a manger because there was no room for them in the inn. They were visited by shepherds who were guided to the manger by angels and by wise men from the East who were guided to the manger by a star. They brought gifts to the babe. These wise men had first gone to see the king to enquire of the birth of the new king. The king, Herod, asked them to return to him when they found the baby so that he too could go to worship him. The wise men became aware of King Herod's intentions, so they did not return to report to the king. An angel advised Joseph to take the mother and baby to Egypt. King Herod, when he saw that he had been deceived by the wise men, was exceedingly angry, and he sent forth and put to death all the male children who were in Bethlehem and in all its surrounding districts, from two years old and under.[35]*

---

35 Summarized from Matt. 1-2.

Buck Responds to the Story

When I identified with this story of the birth of Jesus, my thoughts came out in poetry. Quickly, I got it: King Herod is my ego, and the baby Jesus is my magical inner child. And in my subconscious, the baby Jesus and the baby Moses are the same. Here is what rushed out of me.

Another View of Matthew 2

"What doth lurk there in the bulrushes of my mind?"
"Is it not a babe carefully wrapped in swaddling clothes afloat in a reed basket?"
A magical child,
I hid from myself for fear that I'm not worthy of taking responsibility for its survival and growth.
Yes, it is mine and mine alone, born only of my genes, my unique and solitary thought.
I am its virgin mother.
Yes, I too am a Virgin Mary.
Did not the Holy Spirit lie with me on the night of its conception?
Did not the Three Wise Kings come with their gifts: the myrrh of birth time, the frankincense of birthplace, and the gold of Divine Mother's love?
I've hidden this child from King Herod,
Who also lives most jealously within my mind.
A killer is he—and so well-disguised.
My true love, Joseph—husband, divine will, and hope—will take my hidden child and me to Egypt.
I want this child to know the great mysteries that were denied to me in the modern schools that taught:
"If it can't be measured, then it doesn't exist."
King Herod is the principal of that school.
He has already killed a thousand of my under-two-year-old pals with boyish ideas, but not this one.

This one is the messiah who will one day rescue me from the ravages of
    King Ego Herod,
So I must have this babe educated by those much wiser and braver than I.
He must then be set free to return and liberate me from myself.
Yes, my messiah is coming!
And I am he!

Who Am I?

Jesus is me looking for God.
Christ is me finding God within.
The Holy Child is me in my original innocence.
The Savior is me, fully initiated and still in my original innocence.
And King Herod: Who is he? My Ego, trying to control all the above with
    audacious behaviors.

Buck Explains his Experience of this Story

We begin rereading the gospels from our new point of view. We started with the first New Testament book, Matthew, and with the story of the birth of Jesus. I read the story from the viewpoint that I was every character in the story. This shifted my view of Jesus. Meanwhile, I went to Fiji to study at the Oneness University. I began to understand the impact of the oneness training on how I was experiencing my world. One important early oneness teaching is to experience divine presence as a real person inside us.

Eight months passed before I realized the full impact of this change. Early one morning, while sitting in meditation, I became aware of the presence of someone sitting beside me. As I focused my attention on this presence, I suddenly realized that it is none other than Jesus himself. Well, as someone who hadn't believed in the Christian teaching about Jesus for a long time, I was taken aback. Nonetheless, I had no doubt that the one beside me was indeed Jesus. Then the realization hit me: "He really is a spiritual teacher.

He really does come into people's lives. Here He is in my life right now! Furthermore, He is not something separate from me. I am He." In retrospect, this experience allowed me to understand for the first time the story in the New Testament of the conversion of Paul on the road to Damascus[36]. My conversion to recognizing Jesus as who He claimed to be was as sudden and as unexpected as Paul's.

For the next several days, I cried a lot. My lifelong dilemma was instantly dissolved. My tears were tears of joy, and I was happier than I'd ever been before in my life. I was saved from Christianity, yet I still could have and did have a very personal relationship with Jesus! Thus I became an experientially based Christian.

Again poetry began to arise spontaneously in me.

The Morning Bells

In Martinez Town,
Bells ring at 6:00 every morning,
Bells from an old Catholic church
A few blocks away from my garden.
I wait here each morning to hear their call,
For it is God saying, "Come sit with me awhile,
And tell me what your heart wants to say,
For I love you and listen to your every word.
Say to me whatever you need to say,
For I love unconditionally
And will always respond to you in Truth,
Never judging,
For I am not *the God of the tree of the knowledge of good and evil;*
I am the God of the tree of life."

My Jesus, I have found you after a lifetime of searching,
Shoveling through so many blasphemous words called the Words of God,
And so many of these words were not really your words,
Yet your words were there too,

---

36 Acts 9:1–6

Carefully hidden amongst good and evil distracters
Of that old and judgmental God.
Not you, the God of Love, but him:
The God of Judgments, demanding sacrifices,
    The God of Abraham
    And Crucifixions.
But You, oh God of Love,
    God of Understanding and Compassion,
    God of Jesus
    And unconditional Love.

Yes, my Jesus, they hid you so well that I thought I'd never find you,
But these beloved bells called me to you.
And now I know that Jesus, you and I are one.

My Jesus

My Jesus is not a marble statue behind the altar,
Nor a dead nude on a cross,
Nor the One so often misrepresented in that Old Book.
He is the One, on his knees, beside me when I pray
And meditate.

In the oneness training, we are instructed to talk to the divine presence as we would talk to our best friend. Now I was finally feeling that I was succeeding in doing this. We were also instructed to have a personal relationship with this Presence in whatever face of the Divine works best for us. We were taught that the divine might have more than one image.

For several years, I have been doing a meditation in which I visualize inviting divine beings to join me. I imagine a sacred circle that often includes Jesus, Hiawatha, Nanak, Quetzalcoatl, a Sufi master, an old Arabian man,[37] and others—sometimes Mary Magdalene and

---

37 The Arabian man said nothing, but he continued to be present every morning. One day, I turned to him and asked, "Why are you here?" He responded that it was

Sophia, the Goddess of Divine Wisdom. One day, I went into the sacred circle, expecting to see the usual characters, but all I saw was their bones. So I decided: "OK. Let's just see what happens." But nothing happened, except this same thing kept occurring on a daily basis. But one day, later into the meditation, Jesus showed up. He stood directly in front of me and turned his back to me, then in an instant, He was inside my heart. Hiawatha then did the same maneuver. Then after a week or so, Nanak also entered my heart. And now they are always in my heart.

Once this occurred, the intention of my meditation and inner rituals changed. They are no longer just about me; they are about humankind in general. The intention of these meditations has become the evolution of all human consciousness.

Virginia's Comments

Buck immediately made the jump into experiencing the birth of Jesus within himself and saw the birth of Jesus as an Everyman journey. This means that the allegorical truth and mystical applications of the story apply to us all. We have only to realize this for ourselves. We saw that the baby Jesus represents the sacred child in each of us, the child of innocence and truth. Within each of us is that part of us that knows the truth of life, and when we discover it, we exclaim: Ah-ha! The sacred child is the part of us that hungers after the truth of life and of our lives.

If we will trust our sacred child, he/she will lead us to higher consciousness and acknowledge who we are. This spiritual knowledge can then teach us, heal us, guide us, and energize us to change our world. The ego, represented in the story by King Herod, does not want to give up control to the sacred child, so in the story, King Herod tries to kill the child. The ego wants to kill the desire for spiritual things that the sacred child represents. Our ego and the sacred child oppose each other.

---

because his people needed to hear the message of this book more than the Christians. He was here to encourage us to publish this book in Arabic.

78

Just as Jesus lived a life of compassion and love, so our sacred child can lead us to that life. Living that life requires possessing knowledge of ourselves and a love of ourselves. As we understand the hurts and wounds of our lives, we can heal ourselves, just as Jesus healed all those who were brought to him.

Our ego is constantly making comparisons between ourselves and others, which makes us feel good or bad about ourselves because we are not like them; we are better or worse. Our ego tries to make life a competition between ourselves and others in our lives.[38] The ego wants us to feel good about ourselves because we are better than others. This classic dualism is the result of the ascendancy of the ego, and as we release our dependency on the ego and trust our sacred child, we find that a new world can emerge in which we can live a Christ-like life.

Giving up on the ego and trusting the sacred child is a learned spiritual discipline. Just as Jesus and his family went to Egypt for training and knowledge, returned to Palestine, and continued the training of Jesus, so we can learn to live in a nondualistic world of oneness. Just as Jesus began his earthly ministry with his baptism, we too can begin a spiritual ministry once we have released the ego and trusted our life to our compassionate self. In being healed from our emotional hurts and wounds of the past, we can truly love ourselves. Out of that love, we can allow ourselves to love others and for them to love us.

Many of the spiritual disciplines and religions in the world give us patterns or processes by which we can eliminate the ego and seek higher consciousness. In Christianity, this is commonly taught by teaching new Christians to pray and to memorize verses in the Bible, as well as by making one's life conform to the ways in which other Christians behave. This cloning process usually has the effect of strengthening the ego rather than decreasing our reliance on it. This is because the foundation of this process is comparison and judgment: Judgment of oneself and judgment of others. This dualism is rooted

---

38 Wilfrid R. Konopen adds this comment: "It's not all positive, sometimes, the ego can stir up envy, insecurity, rage, jealousy, ect; it's not all 'I'm better than your are' (although that one is more fun for the ego than the flip side of the coin).

in the tree of the knowledge of good and evil. Western Civilization has operated under this dualistic cloud for centuries. This dualism has produced war and has destroyed our sense of responsibility for our environment. It has produced greed and selfishness. Only as we stop judging ourselves and others can we rise to higher consciousness.

We found that experiencing the allegorical meaning of the birth of Jesus and applying that meaning to our lives became an initiation. Through this life lesson, we can evolve into a higher consciousness. In realizing how our ego parallels King Herod in the story, our ego is exposed as the traitor and murderer that it is. The ego is a traitor because it keeps us from the evolution of our spirit, and it is a murderer because it continually sabotages our holiness. In realizing this, we automatically move into an awareness of ourselves that is helpful in attaining higher consciousness.

Several problems arise from interpreting the story of Jesus literally. The literal meaning is that Jesus, the Son of God, was born to take away the sins of the world. Firstly, this literal interpretation supports and encourages the belief that God is out there, detached from you and me. Secondly, it removes the responsibility of right living away from you and me, placing it onto the God who died so that we might be saved. Thirdly, for salvation, I now project my awareness out there to Jesus for salvation, rather than making the wonderful journey to Christ consciousness within. The message from the sacred child is that this hope is within ourselves.

So when Buck read the story of the birth of Jesus in Matthew, he experienced his sacred child and wrote a poem about the experience. It was real to him because he internalized the truth of the sacred child being born and exalted in each of us. Buck then personalized this insight to his journey.

Conclusion

This story beautifully illustrates the warring within us of our ego and the sacred part of us that longs for enlightenment. The ego of dualism even tries to persuade us that oneness is absurd, that separateness is true reality. The ego tries to make us believe us that oneness is a fairy tale. Just as King Herod tried to kill the baby Jesus, so the ego tries to kill our God consciousness. Oneness takes salvation out from under ego's rule. In the state of oneness, the ego is irrelevant. The ego is powerless to affect our psyche or its decisions and emotions.

In the ancient treatise by Ngulchu Gyalsas Thogmed Zangpo (1245–1369), *The 37 Practices of the Bodhisattva*, we read the fourteenth through the seventeenth practices. This is what happens in the life of those whose ego is irrelevant.

Fourteenth Practice

If, without reason, certain people slander us to the point at which the entire world is filled with their malicious gossip, to praise their virtues lovingly is a practice of a Bodhisattva.

Fifteenth Practice

If in the company of several people, one among them reveals a fault that we would have liked to have kept hidden, to not become irritated with the one who treats us in this manner, but to consider him as a supreme guru is a practice of the Bodhisattva.

Sixteenth Practice

If someone whom we have helped and protected as our own child shows only ingratitude and dislike in return, to behave toward this person with the tender pity a mother has for her sick child is a practice of the Bodhisattva.

Seventeenth Practice

If someone who is your equal or someone who is obviously your inferior despises you or out of arrogance attempts to debase you, to respect him as your master is a practice of the Bodhisattva.

Can Christians be Saved?

Jesus also talked a lot about this issue. "Blessed are you when people insult you, persecute you, and falsely say all kinds of evil against you because of me [your spiritual nature]"[39]. Practices to quiet the ego can be found in any of the traditional spiritual practices, such as mindfulness, meditation, and chants. In the next story are rituals and intentions that render the ego powerless.

The Three Temptations of Jesus

Parable *After Jesus was baptized, He was led up by the Spirit into the wilderness to be tempted by the devil. And when He had fasted forty days and forty nights, afterward He was hungry.*

The devil says to Jesus	*Jesus replies:*
1. *If thou be the Son of God, command that these stones be made bread.*	*"It is written: Man shall not live by bread alone, but by every word that proceedeth out of the mouth of God."*
2. *If thou be the Son of God, cast thyself down: for it is written, "He shall give his angels charge concerning thee: and in their hand they shall bear thee up, lest at any time thou dash thy foot against a stone."*	*"Thou shalt not tempt the Lord thy God."*
3. *All these things I will give thee, if thou wilt fall down and only shalt worship me.*	*Thou shall worship the Lord thy God, and Him thou serve."*

Then the devil left Him, and behold, angels came and ministered to Him.[40]

---

39 Matthew 5:11
40 Matt. 4:4–10.

82

Buck Speaks

It took me a while to get into this allegory, but by letting my true self address my ego as the devil, the revelation emerged as poetry. Virginia later added the final stanza to this poem.

The Three Temptations

First Temptation: Make a rock into bread

Oh Great Ego,
You can wear the mask of the devil,
Devour my golden willpower,
And make me eat a rock as if it were bread.

Second Temptation: Jump from the top of the
temple and let God save me

Oh Great Ego,
You can blind me from my inner seeing,
Preventing me from knowing God within,
And make me demand salvation from something external.

Third Temptation: Allow myself to have power over all

Oh Great Ego,
If I give you permission,
You'd have me fall in lust
For power over everything.

Virginia Speaks

Oh Great Ego,
How can I make you small?
Does it take a wilderness experience
To see you brought low?

Can Christians be Saved?

I was preparing to do a death–rebirth ritual, and I was studying death and my acceptance of my own death and death in general. One night during this process, I had a dream: I go down to visit Ereshkigal, the Queen of the Dead, in the Underworld. In the Myth of the "Descent of Inanna" (see appendix), Inanna, Queen of the Earth, goes down to visit her sister in the Underworld, and Ereshkigal kills Inanna. Later, Inanna is rescued, and we tell of a ritual involving this myth later in this book. But as I journey (in my dream) down to visit Ereshkigal, I am aware that she personifies evil in the dualistic system.

When I arrive in the Underworld, a ritual is being performed with several of my closest friends, and Ereshkigal is spouting curses on my friends. She says, "I am the keeper and creator of death and life, I hold the keys of death, and you dare to come here. Who are you, unless you are some sort of adolescent observers of that which you do not know? You desert your hope by coming here. Here is only despair and hopelessness. You useless rabble of bones, you group of do-nothings, you tire me by even seeing your faces."

She then turns toward me, and I know that she wants me to join or unite or be in union with her. As our two consciousnesses come together, I am horrified. I am joining with her and shouting curses at my friends. I start to resist, but I'm also beginning to experience Ereshkigal's feelings. A deep sorrow comes into me, along with strong jealousy and hatred. She/I feel very bitter that she is the Queen of the Underworld, while her sister Inanna is the Queen of the beautiful Earth above. In an instant, I understand where her rage originates.

I am being summoned from within her to experience her true creative powers. We began prophesying good things for my friends, words of healing and peace, and she releases them. I then separate from her, and she looks me in the eye with wonder. The dream ends.

Around a week later, I am given the interpretation of the dream in a journey. My higher self allows Ereshkigal to sit with me. Together, we discern the interpretation of the dream. Ereshkigal says, "The union of you and me means that you, Virginia, have lost your pretense of innocence, while I have lost my fury. You saw that you and I

84

were one and that I am bitterness, hatred, and murder. I kill children, and I feel my rage, even my own death. At first, you were horrified and did not want to be a part of the curses that I was shouting at each of your friends in your dream. But then, you realized that you and I were one and that you had become what you despised in yourself and what you feared. In becoming me, your ego became useless. Your ego has always wanted to rise above others and establish its own territory. Your ego required separateness so that recognition could come to it and to you. But if you are both death and life, both bitterness and love, both murderess and savior, then your ego has nothing to do. It only has power if there is the separateness created by good and evil, through which the ego can judge itself to be good, thereby elevating itself above others whom it has judged to be bad. When you surrender your ego's need to prove something, then you are free, and your ego becomes irrelevant. Your ego loses its importance.

"You gained innocence in your acceptance of your wholeness, while I lost my fury with you. I used to scream at you. I would scream curses, warnings, and awful stories of fear, while you would resist me. You would not listen. Instead, you would practice your Zen, and I could rarely get through, although I kept trying. Now, however, my fury has abated. There is no use screaming at you anymore. For your ego has lost its power, and there is no root in you to hear or echo my fury. I lost my power over you when you, Virginia, realized that I was your mirror."

As I returned to this dream with this knowledge, I realized the incredible difference between the dualistic world and the world of oneness. In dualism, one cannot be God because God is out there and is the all-powerful Creator of the world. But in oneness, I am God, and you are God. All people are challenged to have this realization; this is the God position, and we are complete when we realize that God is in all and is ALL. The kingdom of heaven is within. But in oneness, I am also the devil or Ereshkigal. However, I am not the dualistic devil who commits crazy acts of evil; I am conscious of my oneness with all things. This has to include the things that are called the opposite of good. That does not mean that my behavior will reflect what we call evil, but it does mean that the capacity for and the understanding of such things dwells in us all. Evil only loses its power over us as we admit that it is there and embrace it. By becoming Ereshkigal, I know that I could never claim to be any better than anyone else. It is simply that I am a human, the same as anyone who has made choices to see the world enlightened, while others on this earth have made choices to make decisions according to their desires, suffer in this life, and cause others to suffer.

Furthermore, I also know that no one is better than I am. This statement seems preposterous to a dualistic mind because the ego teaches us that there are saints here now (and were long ago) who are (were) much better than we are. But oneness says that they and I are one; I have the capacity and the understanding to do acts of compassion, just as we all do. I can choose to make decisions that reflect understanding and compassion.

Oneness is the foundation by which we can have an operating system (in computer language) that is virus-free. Upon this foundation, we can make decisions to have love and compassion for our world and for our neighbor.

Once I considered that the dualistic judgments of my ego were irrelevant, I rested from my labors of trying to kill the ego and entered the world where all things are possible. So I say, "My holiness envelops the world."[41] I say that as a statement of fact, not as a dualistic statement that I am any holier than anyone else. Those comparisons have become meaningless to me.

Virginia Concludes

In this story, we find pathways to oneness and higher consciousness. If we put ourselves in the place of Jesus, we see that temptations always come to us when we are weak or when our attention is diverted from our spiritual path. Think back to times of temptations in your own life. When I did so, I immediately remembered times when I gave into a temptation and paid a price for doing so. Remembering times when I resisted temptation is much harder.

41 *A Course in Miracles*, Workbook lesson #36.

Why is this? Maybe my old ego didn't like not being in charge and so refused to let memory function.

In my life, overcoming the ego has focused on removing from my mind the tendency to compare myself with others. In my life, my thoughts have often been about making comparisons with others; my thoughts have been egocentric. My thoughts of judgment of others reinforced my ego and told me how great I was. "Thank God that I am not like that poor person," I would think. "Thank God I am not like that carjacker," I would say. "Thank God I do not think like George W. Bush," I would say. All thoughts such as this show me how wrong the world is and how right I am, how much better than others I am.

Studying nonjudgment is my greatest key to realizing that my thoughts immerse me in the world of duality, and that as I judge others, I truly am judging myself. In my struggle to overcome the ego, I discovered one day that the only way to escape the ego is to render it useless and irrelevant. This is how I realized this.

The Parables

Introduction

> **The Story** *"He who has ears, let him hear." The disciples came to Jesus and asked, "Why do you speak to the people in parables?" He replied, "The knowledge of the secrets of the kingdom of heaven has been given to you, but not to them."*[42]

Jesus

My heart lives in more than one dimension and speaks a different language in each dimension. What I say to the inner parts of myself would make little sense if spoken to the public. However, I do have some friends so near and dear to

---

42 Matthew 12:12–14.

me that I can speak to them as I speak to my self. These dear friends are you.

There may be those of you who will be able to invite me into your heart. When you do, then you then be able to hear me. The key to becoming the one: *"He who has ears, let me hear"* is for you to experience yourself as me. And when you can experience yourself as me, then you will be able to live and understand my stories Jesus:. The secret knowledge is that the kingdom of heaven is in our oneness with each other. In time, you too may learn this secret, but for now, for many people, their judgmental thinking precludes this realization.

—Buck as Jesus

What are these parables to us as we explore the gospels? Suppose that they have a special message for each of us. Suppose we contemplate them with the intention to discover a specific new insight for ourselves. Can you let go of judgment and become a mustard seed, a good Samaritan, and the unforgiving servant? Each parable likely holds a unique secret for each of us.

The Mustard Seed

Parable *"The kingdom of heaven is like to a grain of mustard seed, which a man took, and sowed in his field: Which indeed is the least of all seeds, but when it is grown, it is the greatest among herbs, and becometh a tree, so that the birds of the air come and lodge in the branches thereof."*[43]

And when he was demanded of the Pharisees, when the kingdom of God should come, he answered them and said, "The kingdom of God cometh not with

---

43   Matt. 13:31–32

observation: Neither shall they say, Lo here! or, lo there! for, behold, the kingdom of God is within you."[44]

Jesus answered, "I tell you the truth, no one can enter the kingdom of God (heaven) unless he is born of water and the Spirit. Flesh gives birth to flesh, but the Spirit gives birth to spirit. You should not be surprised at my saying, 'You must be born again.'"[45] "

Another parable spake he unto them, "The kingdom of heaven is like unto leaven, which a woman took, and hid in three measures of meal, till the whole was leavened."[46]

Buck Speaks

As I contemplated this parable and the other ideas about heaven attributed to Jesus, a memory surfaced. One night, I was lying on top of a mountain in southern New Mexico. There was no moon-light, nor any source of artificial light. In my mind's eye, I return to this place. I see infinite blackness, dotted with countless stars or points of light that shine down on me. These points of light now seem to represent points of consciousness, like those of many mas-ters who have found themselves to be in the God position: the sons and daughters of God. These infinite sources of light are there in the unlimited vastness of space. These light sources all shine on me, bless me, and invite me to enter into the silence with them. I rec-ognize that the silence is this empty vastness between the points of light. I now rest within this vastness, this silence and this shower of blessings from so many sacred companions. It feels heavenly. I become aware that Nanak, the first Sikh guru, is one of these points of light, and I am reminded of Nanak's teaching that truth is the name of God and that truth is found in silence. I bask in Nanak's

---

44 Luke 17:20–21
45 John 3:5–7
46 Matt. 13:33

blessing and his wisdom. I also do this with Jesus, Hiawatha, and many other great teachers.

I too am also a point of light; I am the tiny mustard seed, a small perception that grows to include everything in all of Creation. I am the pinch of leaven that permeates the whole loaf. This heaven is vast, yet it is this tiny vision inside my inner eye in my imagination. Now I realize the truth of the old adage: "As above, so below." Heaven is vast and everywhere; paradoxically, it is also tiny and inside me.

Before this, I had studied some Huna teaching of the Hawaiians. One of their concepts has been very useful to me: We have three parts to our souls: the *uhani*, the manager or the decision maker that includes the ego; the *unihipili*, the inner child self or subconscious; and the *aumakua*, our higher consciousness. As a result of this vision, I began to experience my *aumakua* as totally within the Divine. Another way of saying this is that the will of God and my will are the same. This is the will of my *aumakua*, not the schemes of my ego! The space of my *aumakua* and that of all others within the will of God seems to sum up to the Akashic Records, the infinite celestial library in which all human knowledge resides. This suggests that when I am truly within the vastness of the *aumakua* of all beings, I should have access of this storehouse of wisdom. This is part of my experience of being in the kingdom of heaven.

Virginia's Conclusion

Buck's vision is a good example of a meditation that leads to a visualization of oneness. When we look at our world, it appears to contain separate beings, but meditation helps us to be able to see the world in oneness, not the illusion of separateness. Looking at the vast and infinite points of light in the vision, considering that each one represents a point of consciousness, is a wonderful practice for expanding our vision of the world. When we consider that universal consciousness is available to us through personal spiritual teachers or through accessible universal wisdom, we realize how truly blessed we are. The next parable is also a lesson in the oneness of our earth family.

The Good Samaritan

> *Parable*: Jesus answered, "A certain man was going down from Jerusalem to Jericho, and he fell among robbers, who both stripped him and beat him, and departed, leaving him half dead. By chance, a certain priest was going down that way. When he saw him, he passed by on the other side. In the same way, a Levite also, when he came to the place and saw him passed by on the other side. But a certain Samaritan, as he traveled, came where he was. When he saw him, he was moved with compassion, came to him, and bound up his wounds, pouring on oil and wine. He set him on his own animal, brought him to an inn, and took care of him. On the next day, when he departed, he took out two denarii, gave them to the host, and said to him, 'Take care of him. Whatever you spend beyond that, I will repay you when I return.' Now which of these three do you think seemed to be a neighbor to him who fell among the robbers?" He said, "He who showed mercy on him." Then Jesus said to him, "Go and do likewise."[47]

Virginia Speaks

I am riding my bike and pass a homeless person who is vomiting in the storm drain on the side of the road. I pass him by, but after going a half a block, I am still thinking about him. I wonder whether I should turn around and offer my assistance to him. After thinking about this for a second, I ignore him and continue my bike ride. "What could I have done?" I do not know, but I missed my chance to find out. Why did I not stop? At the very least, I could have tried to comfort him for a moment.

---

47 Luke 10:30–37

There was a time in my life when I invariably answered a call to help a person who needed help. For several years, I corresponded with a transgender person in prison. Her name was Cindy. I learned about her life, and she learned about my life. We shared letters every other month or so.

One day, I got a call from her attorney, who told me that she was ready to be released, but first she had to find a place to stay. Her mother was willing to pay the prisoner's rent after release, but the ex-convict had to find a place to live before the authorities would release her. The attorney explained that several attempts had been made to rent an apartment for her, but when the owners found out it was for a person from prison, they refused to rent to her.

The attorney asked me to help Cindy find a place to live. At the time, I had an empty apartment out back, a perfect space for her. It had a bath and a large studio space. But I wondered, "Do I want to rent to a person out on parole?"

As I investigated Cindy's history, I discovered nothing to comfort me. Cindy, while she had been living as a man, had been very violent. She had spent most of her adult life in prison, the last sentence being for second-degree murder. She was completing her sentence of ten years. She had committed other murders and perpetrated other crimes. Cindy had not only a violent past, but also a violent nature. For several days, I mulled it over, going back and forth on whether I should rent to her. The decision boiled down to one problem. I was afraid that her violent tendencies would continue, that if I let her stay in my back apartment on my property, I might be in danger.

I remembered the parable. If I had compassion for her, would I not help? Hadn't I been corresponding with her all this time? In spite of my fear, I agreed to accept that I might be hurt or killed, but I would be doing the right thing in this moment and that I could not control what might happen tomorrow. Later, I told several friends of my decision. They admired my courage, even though I could see that they thought that I had made a mistake.

Cindy arrived and stayed for two years. At the end of her parole and probation period, she moved into a place of her own. Now, several years later, she is doing well and staying clean and free. She still tells me that I am her savior, and no one else would have helped her. My actions gave her another chance at life.

As I look back on that decision to help Cindy, it was a wonderful thing for both of us. She got her new chance, and I gained a friend. This would not have happened unless I had been able to see past my fears and let my compassion in that moment allow me to help her. Since then, I think I have been able to recognize folks needing help, and I have been able to help many people. But I still encounter the occasional situation in which I find myself identifying with the very important persons in the parable who walked on by the injured man because they were too busy, too good, or too afraid to help. When this happens, I am reminded not to judge those whom I feel are not compassionate because they and I are one and the same. This recognition of my nonduality may be the highest lesson of the parable. Judgment of others becomes impossible in the light of the realization of my own humanity and divinity.

Where is the Good Samaritan?

I am checking out at Wal-Mart. The clerk is subtly expressing a hidden pain. I see her name on her name tag and ask her by name: "How are you?" Expressing pain with her eyes, she explains that she is not feeling well. She puts her hand on her neck or shoulder, indicating that she needs relief from a painfully twisted muscle. An inner voice says to me that if I place my hands on her neck and shoulder as do the Kuhuna healers of Hawaii, she will get the relief that she needs. "But," I think, "here in Wal-Mart, in the front of the store, most likely there will be a supervisor looking on." After a brief pause, I walk on, feeling ashamed of my reluctance and fear. I rejected my opportunity to be a good Samaritan. But I held

**onto my invitation to feel ashamed of my timidity.
I hope that I've learned my lesson.**

—Buck

Conclusion by Virginia

On recalling this parable, it is easy for us to get the lesson—until we are walking through our daily lives and observing our actions, when we may ignore many folk who need our help. Usually this is because it is inconvenient for us, given our busy schedules; we may feel unsafe if we engage a person enough to help; or we are thinking about other things and unaware of the person's situation. Why do we do this? Often, this is an automatic response resulting from a dualistic view of our world and the separation that it causes.

The awareness of nonduality may begin with just one person with whom we are in contact. As we push through those prejudices, fears, and inattention to help and bless another person, the dualistic world disintegrates, leaving us free to express love and compassion. When one practices this repeatedly, the walls of separation grow thin.

When I think about the good Samaritan, I tend to think of him as a good neighbor, something I often heard preachers call him in my past. The question I ask is: "Who is my neighbor?" My reply from a oneness point of view is that all those who need my help and compassion are my neighbors. Furthermore, no one who belongs to a certain group, ethnicity, or nationality is unworthy of my help, love, and compassion.

Buck's story is a great example of something that almost all have experienced: regret at not having helped another. The lesson here is to forgive ourselves quickly, to take compassion even for ourselves, and to know that even in oneness, there is no dogma ("No, you shouldn't have done that!"). There is only our natural state: to bless all, even ourselves. A pathway to oneness is found in blessing others; in doing so, we also bless ourselves.

The Unforgiving Servant

*If we practice an eye for an eye and a tooth for a tooth,
soon the whole world will be blind and toothless.*

Mahatma Ghandi

Parable: *Therefore the kingdom of heaven is like a certain king, who wanted to reconcile accounts with his servants. When he had begun to reconcile, one was brought to him who owed him ten thousand talents. But because he couldn't pay, his lord commanded him to be sold, with his wife, his children, and all that he had, and payment to be made. The servant therefore fell down and kneeled before him, saying, "Lord, have patience with me, and I will repay you all!" The lord of that servant, being moved with compassion, released him, and forgave him the debt. But that servant went out and found one of his fellow servants, who owed him one hundred denarii, and he grabbed him and took him by the throat, saying, "Pay me what you owe!" So his fellow servant fell down at his feet and begged him, saying, "Have patience with me, and I will repay you!" He would not, but went and cast him into prison, until he should pay back that which was due. So when his fellow servants saw what was done, they were exceedingly sorry and came and told to their lord all that was done. Then his lord called him in, and said to him, "You wicked servant! I forgave you all that debt because you begged me. Shouldn't you also have had mercy on your fellow servant, even as I had mercy on you?" His lord was angry and delivered him to the tormentors until he should pay all that was due to him. So my heavenly Father will also do to you, if you don't each forgive your brother from your hearts for hismisdeeds."[48]*

---

48 Matt. 18:23–35

Can Christians be Saved?

Virginia Speaks

In 1997, I visited a gay church for the first time. Having a conservative Christian background, I had always been involved with spiritual things and had even served as pastor of several conservative churches in the early 1980s. I had recently gotten divorced, and I was questioning whether I was gay. I had always felt different from other boys and men, but I had never had a sexual experience with another man. I had many questions, and I was going to the gay church mostly to observe and to check out any message that might be there for me.

Upon entering the front, I realized that I was early, so I walked over to a table of literature and begin to read the titles: "You are Gay and Loved by God" and "Is the Homosexual my Neighbor?" and "Homosexuality is not a Sin." I thumbed through them and picked up some free ones to read later. At the end of the table I find a newspaper called *The Second Stone* and noticed an article entitled "Baptist Pastor kept no secrets." This interested me because my father was a Baptist minister, and I grew up in Southern Baptist churches. The first line of the piece had the words "Henry Finch."

In 1962, when I was eleven, my father was the pastor of the First Baptist Church of Salisbury, North Carolina. He hired an assistant pastor who had recently graduated from the Baptist seminary: Henry Finch, the only man whom as a boy I had sworn to hate.

Henry was good-looking, friendly, and dynamic. He spent time with the youth of the church. Several years after he was hired in Salisbury, my father let him preach every Sunday night. As expected, some people in the church wanted to hear the young preacher, even though they usually did not attend the evening service. One night, in 1963 or 1964, here in the Deep South, Henry preached a sermon that supported the civil rights movement and the integration of Southern institutions. The next day, my father took me to see Henry's car, which had been firebombed in the early hours of the morning. One side of the car was a blackened charred mess. I commented to Dad about how horrible this was. "He shouldn't have preached that sermon," my father replied.

I loved and respected my father. He preached to almost a thousand people every Sunday. I wanted to be like him. But when he disapproved of Henry's sermon, I knew that Dad wasn't seeing the issue of civil rights clearly. I was confused by my father's condemnatory statement. I thought that it was important to speak one's truth, whatever the cost.

I also remember traveling with Henry Finch to Washington, DC, with about twelve boys from my church. I rode in Henry's car, and I remember the four boys who rode with Henry having a tickling battle in the car while he drove. Henry seemed to egg us on, and he really enjoyed our company on the drive up and back.

But the thing that seared him in my memory was my saying that I hated him. That was 1967, and my father had been forced to resign from the pastorate there at First Church. I never got the complete story of how this came to be; I only know that a group of men in the church did not like the way Dad preached. Maybe they did not like the way he ran certain things in the church. Factions developed, power struggles ensued, and rather than fight the factions and cause a potential church split, my father resigned. Later, my parents told me that Henry Finch had been instrumental in turning some people against Dad, even though Henry had left in 1966 for another church. My parents blamed Henry for Dad's problems. Not knowing any reason why I should question my parents, I hated Henry for that. Several months after we left North Carolina, my best friend there, Rusty Porter, was killed in an automobile accident. I decided to return to Salisbury for the funeral, as I had been chosen to be a pallbearer. Rusty's father drove me to the church that day, and I asked him who was officiating at the funeral. "Why Henry Finch is," he said to me.

"I hate him for what he did to my father," I said.

Mr. Porter seemed shocked at my statement. He replied, "Billy, you should not hate anyone. Do not hate Henry."

When we reached the church, I walked up to the casket, which was being brought into the sanctuary. Henry Finch was standing there with a group of men. I gave him the darkest hate-filled look that I could muster. He quickly looked away and went about his business, but I felt very justified.

Thirty years later, as I stood in the lobby of this gay church, remembering the events I have just described, as I read the story of Henry Finch, the Baptist pastor who kept no secrets, I was overcome with excitement, but also with a fearful uncertainty of what I was about to read.

I read that twenty years after Rusty's funeral, Henry had come out as gay to the Southern Baptist church that he was pastoring. He was removed from the ministry and entered a mental institution for a time. Upon release from the hospital, he found a job working at a clinic as a counselor to alcoholics and drug addicts. He became a leader in his community in the fight against AIDS. One of his Southern Baptist pastor friends asked him to teach Sunday school. The pastor, Gene Owens of the Myers Park Baptist Church in Charlotte, North Carolina, said that he didn't care whether Finch was gay. Owens eventually offered Henry a deaconship at the church, which Henry declined. Henry continued to work tirelessly at the clinic until his death as a result of complications from AIDS in 1994. His partner for the last three years of his life was Patrick, who stated that Henry kept in touch with his many friends in the Baptist churches. According to Patrick, all of Henry's friends, including his straight Baptist friends, were supportive. "Henry helped to get my life back on track," Patrick said soon after Henry's death. "I miss him a lot."

As I read these words I realized that the man I had hated all these years seems not to have been the monster I remembered. Instead, Henry was a person such as I, imperfect, but with a desire to do the right thing. As I went into the service at that gay church, I experienced forgiving Henry Finch, after all those years.

In a way, Henry's coming out to freedom in his life to be who he was resulted in my freedom from the bitterness of hate as I read the story of his life. That experience held a strong lesson for me that the things that we do may have a great effect on others. Forgiveness sets people free. I did not want to retain the attitude within me of the unforgiving servant, with all the baggage of the judgmental Old Testament God of Wrath.

Buck Speaks

"I'm going to make sure that you never get to see your daughter again." Those were my wife's parting words as she moved out at the start of our third and final separation before the divorce. To make things worse, she entered the house one day when I was at work, took everything of value, and left a terrific mess. What she didn't take was thrown around, dumped out, and trashed. The most disgusting was a pot full of fermenting fruit that she had dumped onto the cabinet top, which producing a distinct and sickeningly sweet odor that pervaded the house for weeks.

This occurred in Maryland, where the laws were particularly unfavorable to a father's visitation rights. What followed were months of struggle to get my visitation rights with my daughter.

One summer, after arrangements had been made for me to pick up my daughter from summer camp so that I could be with her for my allotted two weeks of summer vacation, my daughter called. She said that her mother was coming to pick her up. If that happened, I wouldn't get to see my daughter. I was at work and didn't have my car, so I asked a friend to take me immediately to the camp to pick up my daughter. We got there just as my ex and her lover were driving away with my daughter. We followed, trying to get them to stop, but they only drove faster and faster. The chase continued through the winding Maryland country roads, while my daughter in the back of their car waved to us. Finally, I said to my friend, "Please stop." I didn't want this wild chase to cause anyone's death. I did not get my visit with my daughter. This caused my anger with my ex to increase.

Now that my daughter is an adult, I do actually get to see her most months. But even while she was still a minor, once I started taking her to weekly riding lessons, I got to see her more often. The exchanges between my ex and me, however, never did become pleasant.

Anger and hatred for my ex haunted me for years until one day I realized that my feelings were hurting no one but me. So I decided simply to release my anger and forgive her. I took a deep breath and let go of my anger. Now, when I see her, we can speak amicably.

Conclusion—Virginia Speaks

Leaving aside all of the literal interpretations, this parable is about one thing: forgiveness. When we forgive someone, we are free of the entanglements and mind chatter that holding onto anger and resentment produces. When we harbor lack of forgiveness, toxic thoughts are produced: negative or hateful thoughts of the one who wronged us. "How could he (or she) have done such a thing?" we ask ourselves, thereby experiencing the hurt over and over again. The lack of forgiveness forces us to relive the event repeatedly, along with our reaction and emotional response. True forgiveness sets us free from that cycle so that we can love and experience again a compassionate heart. When the person we have forgiven either learns that we have forgiven him or her or is set free simply by the spiritual act of the moment, then that person also experiences freedom.

It is never too late or too early to forgive someone. Sometimes we delay forgiving someone because we want to punish them for a while with our anger and hostility. We might never put it that way, but that is exactly what we do when we harbor lack of forgiveness. Sometimes we get an opportunity to forgive someone who wronged us many years ago, and it sets us free and heals us in the present moment as we experienced in the stories shared above. Lack of forgiveness produces unhealthy spiritual connections between our present self and the objects of our lack of forgiveness. This can cause us to be confused about decisions in the present or not to be able to experience freedom in all areas of our lives. This is especially true of those who we feel justified in not forgiving.

The story of Jesus forgiving from the Cross those who crucified him is an example of the spiritual power of forgiveness. Very important are the relationships with our father, mother, siblings, children, spouses, and former spouses. All of these relationships need to be cleansed with our forgiveness for us to be free in the present.

As one experiences the state of oneness, the need to forgive others does not arise as often because we are not offended as often.

Additional Thought—Buck Speaks

Given that the first and last sentences of the parable follow the Old Testament idea of an "eye for and eye and a tooth for a tooth," one assumption is that these were added by the writer rather that actually being the words of Jesus. Another interpretation is that in this point in his development, Jesus is still confused as to which God he represents. One thing is certain, however: the parable shows the difference between forgiveness and holding onto anger, resentment, and harsh judgments of others.

Synthesis – Virginia Speaks

We selected only four of the many parables in the New Testament. Each provided insightful personal stories. We have been able to identify ourselves in these allegories. However, there are forty parables in the New Testament alone. Thus the sacred literature of our world is rich with these types of teaching stories.

When we have an experience that ungrounds us or that makes us angry or fearful, the experiences with the parables suggest that there are alternative ways of reacting. One way is to accept the experience as a challenge and an invitation to have a new learning experience, one that will evolve our consciousness and lighten our soul. The sacred scriptures are vast sources of such wisdom. We are thus invited to learn our individual truths by experiencing these stories as though they were about us individually and personally.

Another powerful way to utilize these sacred stories is to turn them into initiations—ceremonies for our personal growth by experiencing them dramatically.

✳✳

Chapter 5

Initiations

Introduction: Buck Speaks

Initiations

All this talk of enlightenment and being on a spiritual path!
I prefer to think in terms of initiations.
Once plagued with problems, conflicts, and times of misery,
I now have only invitations[49] to initiations
Into the wisdom provided by these mysteries of life.
I'm not going anywhere;
I'm just being here,
Learning where I am
And watching what I'm doing about it.

---

49 "The tests that we undergo arise as we remove the obstacles within ourselves to hearing the voice of love more clearly. From this perspective, each crisis we meet is a fresh invitation. As we succeed, in small steps, the elation that we discover along the way helps to sustain our resolve." Alexander J. Shaia: *The Hidden Power of the Gospels* (New York, NY: HarperCollins, 2010), p. 72.

We didn't plan it this way, but when we worked on certain of the allegories in the New Testament, what resulted were powerful initiations for ourselves. Other sacred texts also provided us with the ideas for initiations, such as the ancient Babylonian story of Inanna's descent into hell.

At least two kinds of initiations can come into our lives: those that just spontaneously arise as a natural result of our life journeys and those that we bring into being intentionally. Furthermore, it seems there are patterns or sequences of initiations can really help us with our spiritual development. All of the initiations that we report on (except the first one) are based on allegories from sacred texts, mostly the Bible.

William Becomes Virginia

Virginia Speaks

Our life journey sometimes brings us to unexpected places. Initiations brought on by life experiences can be powerful teachers and bring us to new worlds and into new states of being.

I feel a deep sense of wonder as I lie here, looking at my body. I have smooth skin and rounded hips. Wow, I sorta look like a girl! But, I have this penis right here in the middle of all of this girly stuff, and I just can't figure this out. I ask myself whether I want my penis to go away. My answer to my own question is simply, "No." But my curiosity is intense, and I can't explain why I'm having these feelings about my body. (Later on, I'll learn that these feelings I'm having right now will never go away.) While having these curious feelings about my body, I also remember that my parents expect me to be a success. They remind me what success is supposed to be like. It seems strange that my feelings and this idea from my parents are somehow connected. I just can't figure this out either. What I do know is that this feeling of connectedness between these two things is something that I will long remember and think about.

—Virginia as a boy in bed

I was born male. Through the years, I came to realize that I had been born with an inner identity that was female. My struggle through the years to find congruence between my body and my soul or spirit led me to experience a spiritual awakening. The long journey from being William to being Virginia was at times painful and often a wonderful adventure, but it was never boring.

I was adopted into the home of a Southern Baptist minister in the 1950s and raised to be an all-American boy. My parents were like most of their contemporaries in that they assumed that being successful in life meant that one would be what society expected one to be. So as a preacher's kid and a son of parents who valued achievement highly, I was on a fast track to what they called success. The only problem was me. Inside, I believed that I was different from everyone else, and it took half a lifetime for me to figure this out.

I still vividly remember that day, described above, when I was lying in bed looking at my body, which looked so feminine to me. But I put those feelings and thoughts on the back burner for many years.

"Ask, and it will be give; seek, and you will find; knock, and the door will be opened."

—*Jesus*

In the middle 1990s, I finally gave myself permission to find out why I had always felt different from other boys and men. Even though that feeling of being different had always been with me, I had led a typical life: marrying, having two children, establishing a career, buying a house, etc. But now that my wife and I were getting divorced after nineteen years of marriage, I firmly set my mind to find out why I had always felt different and to see where that discovery would lead. I thought at first that my feeling of being different had something to do with homosexuality. I had never had a gay relationship, but I thought that the enduring habit of mine of wearing my mother's clothes, then my sister's, and finally my wife's, might have something to do with being gay. So I began to attend gay events, gay churches, and gay festivals, as much to learn who I was as to meet people.

> "Everything and everyone around you is your teacher."
> —Ken Keyes

Someone suggested to me one day that I do drag, acting and dressing as a woman and performing on stage. The experience felt that I was coming home. I enjoyed doing drag performances for a while, but I knew inside that there was something more going on inside me. I still had not discovered the truth about myself.

My desire to understand who I was led me to a support group at the University of New Mexico Gender Studies Department: a support group for transgender people. *Transgender* is a blanket term that includes cross-dressers, intersexed persons, masculine-appearing women, feminine-appearing men, and transsexuals—those who live in the gender opposite from that of their birth sex. As I sat there that night, listening to the many stories of the people attending, the pieces started to fall into place for me. I came to see that I had a gender identity of female, despite having been born male. This did not mean that I necessarily appeared feminine to the world, but it meant that I felt inside that my true self was feminine and that I had hid this inner femininity from myself and the world all of my life.

> "You create your own reality."
>
> —Jane Roberts

Knowing at last why I had always felt different from other men and boys, I set out to reinvent my life. All my life, I had felt that I possessed some secret, some unknown place that I feared and thought that others also feared. When I came to know who I really was, I felt free for the first time. I began to experiment with presenting gender in a diverse way and also, little by little, to confront hidden fears (mine and others').

The first thing I decided to do was to tell my children. I had always had a good relationship with both of them and had kept communications open, so I decided to tell them first. My daughter Jennifer was seventeen, and she seemed to accept my revelation without any difficulty. My son Josh was fourteen and living with me. He also seemed to accept my decision to live differently, but I noticed that for several weeks after I told him, he seemed quiet and withdrawn.

I took Josh aside one day and asked him whether anything was wrong. He said that he had been worrying about what I had told him. He did not want his friends to know about my gender identity issues because this would embarrass him. So I made an agreement that I would not let any of his friends see me dressed as a female and that I would let him know in advance when I would dress up as a woman so that he would know ahead of time. Immediately, he felt relieved. He said that everything was OK. He said that he knew that I would still be the same person.

Several months later, I was in my room on a Saturday night dressing to go out. Josh entered my room. He said, "Dad, I have one of my friends from school here, and I wondered: Could I bring her back to see you?" I replied, "Josh, I thought you didn't want anyone to know." Then he said, "Oh, no. It's no big deal. I've told everyone!" So he brought his friend into my room, and we talked make-up for a while. Josh has accepted me ever since then.

> *"All that has existed, exists, or will exist*
> *is interconnected and interdependent."*
>
> —*Thich Nhat Hanh*

For several years, I was fine with just dressing as a woman and going out several times a week dressed that way. I found it energizing, exciting, and filled with adventure. One day, I decided to go to Albuquerque's largest mall dressed as a woman. This would be the first time I had ventured out as female during the day.

I am feeling very nervous as I drive up to the mall. Making a conscious decision to relax, I take several deep breaths and begin to experience joy at the freedom I'm giving myself. As I walk up to the mall to enter through a department store, I am feeling my body and the way I am walking; I think, "This is me. My outer appearance matches the way I feel inside. I'm real; I'm really me. And this feels so good."

Walking through this familiar store, my self-confidence is growing. "I'm tall and stately, and I am proud. Anyone who notices me will be lucky to see me as I truly am."

I walk through the store to the central corridor in the center of the mall—the center of the world of women. "I belong to this tribe now," I think.

Now I begin to notice a strange feeling beginning to arise within me, so I stop at the periphery of the food court. I see lines connecting all the people! These lines appear like lines of laser-like light that are connecting everyone within my sight. As I gaze over the scene, my eyes fall on a mother and her child. As I stare at them, I see them not just as they appear in the present moment, but also I see both of them as children, as well as adults. Plus I can feel the interactions that they have had through the years that they have had together—feelings of pain and struggle, as well as feelings of joy and happiness. "I've never experienced such a thing before," I realize. My gaze now drifts to other people, and I began to feel myself connected to them. Suddenly, I am completely overwhelmed by this experience and start to cry.

—Virginia, A New View of the World

"This is your last chance. After this, there is no turning back. You take the blue pill—the story ends, you wake up in your bed and believe whatever you want to believe. You take the red pill—you stay in Wonderland, and I show you how deep the rabbit-hole goes."

—Morpheus, The Matrix

I was deeply moved by the mystical experience I had undergone at the mall (of all places), so I spent that night meditating on what had happened. What was the connection between my gender variance and my experience? What did this mean spiritually for me? Was I beginning to slip from sanity into another world?

Right about this time I had dinner with a close friend, Julian.

Julian and I are sharing dinner as I decide to confide in him and tell him of my experience at the mall. I explain what had happened, my fear that I am alone, and that I think that I'm losing my mind. I ask him for his opinion, and I find his response unforgettable. He says, "Will, you have had a mystical experience that is real and is life-changing. You are not alone. There are many who have had similar experiences. Your experience represents nonduality and the other world within our world. Embrace your experience, learn, and move on to other experiences."

I cannot fully express to Julian how his words have made me feel. But now I feel greatly encouraged and supported by what he has just said to me. This is a drink of water for my thirsty soul, so I say, "Thank you, Julian!"

—Virginia, Am I Jumping Off the
Edge of the Earth?

Over the next several months, I came to see that the experience was representative of all of these things. I was sane, but I was seeing the world in a different way. This experience confirmed for me the spiritual paths that I was experiencing and studying, which taught the sanctity and interconnectedness of all living things and the oneness of the love that permeated life's fabric. I began to see my gender variance as a portal, a window to see cultural assumptions in a different way, and furthermore, to see the nature of reality in a different way. Just as I had allowed my journey to expose the illusion of society's fundamental rules of gender, I saw that there were many other cultural assumptions that supported a false reality of life. This insight elicited excitement and fear in me simultaneously. Indeed, I had taken the red pill!

"You can build your own heaven or hell on earth."

—*John M. Templeton*

The urge I felt to jump off the edge of the earth was moderated by my commitment to negotiate the curves. I had been good at playing with others, but I realized that I now faced a life-changing decision. Crossing genders and living as a woman seemed like a decision that I had made long ago. It was as if I were only now just remembering it. On one hand, I was excited, as I knew that the change for me was not just for the sake of my happiness, but also that it would produce other transformations in the spiritual and emotional realms. On the other hand, I knew that the impending change could cost me everything in the material plane: my job, my money, my houses, and my reputation. But I knew that whatever the cost, it would be worth it to me finally to be true to myself and honest with others. I also knew that on some level, my gender exploration had much to do with my spiritual awakening, although this was more something that I felt or intuited than it was something that I understood.

The overwhelming motivation within me was to be honest with the world. I came to see that living in a masculine role was like living a lie; it just was not who I am. To be honest at long last with all about who I am was a doorway to freedom. The only reason not to go through that doorway was the fear of losing things. I did not realize it at the time, but these fears would lead me to the life initiation.

I decided to do the transition to female at my place of employment, where I had worked for eleven years. I had been a very successful manager and had turned around several companies, making them profitable. I enjoyed a reputation for fairness, responsibility, and integrity. I was well-liked by my employees, customers, and vendors, and I knew that many of them would support me in whatever I chose to do. I also knew that the wholesaling business is a conservative one, being in construction, and that I would certainly face some opposition. If my boss fired me, I knew that the probability was slender of my finding another job that would pay anything close to what I was making.

As I pondered all this, I remembered that Buddha had said in the Four Noble Truths that suffering arises from attachment to desires, and suffering ceases when we are no longer attached to those desires. *Desire* in the West represents all that we want in life. This typically is our possessions and our financial security. By not being dependent on such things or by not trusting in possessions, one can be free from the fear of losing them. Thereby, one can find peace and freedom within oneself instead of through outward things.

Jesus said a similar thing in Matthew[50] when Jesus taught about trusting God and not worrying. Jesus taught this principle by showing that the worry that we have over possessions can be devastating. He taught that we should put our mind on those things that are above. For years, I had paid attention to the Sermon on the Mount, and I have meditated in the Zen Buddhist tradition for years, yet I did not understand nonattachment. But as I considered the cost of my transition and felt the fear rise in my heart over what I would lose, I finally understood.

"Worry achieves nothing and wastes valuable time."

—*John M. Templeton*

I prepared spiritually for the transition by performing rituals around releasing my fear of losing everything. In the course of my meditation, I came to consider all my possessions as already lost. I detached from them and imagined that they were not mine anymore. I realized that even if I lost all of my material possessions and became homeless, I would still endure somehow. As I write these words, I realize that the reader may suffer from incredulity, but to me, experiencing this realization changed my life. I left behind all of those things, and they became unimportant to me. I lost my attachment to them because I made a decision to lose them. When I realized this, I knew that I had also dissolved all of the obstacles that had prevented me from transitioning at work.

I told my district manager that in six months, I would come in dressed as Virginia. I asked him to help me explain the situation to my employees and customers, as we had plenty of time to prepare everyone for this impending transition. Even though he was uncomfortable, he took a wait-and-see attitude. I told my employees. Several of them had a hard time with the information. Some tried to use my situation as an opportunity to move into my position, while others had gender or sexual issues of their own and could not handle

50 Matthew 6:25–34.

my openness about mine. Some had gay family members and in their minds associated me with them. So for several months, I endured emotional confrontations with my employees. I heard what they said and saw the way that they acted.

Initially, several people evidently felt threatened by my announcement of my future action and began to attack me out of their fear. At first, I took their attacks personally. I only saw the good things that I had done for them in the past, so their sudden hostility seemed grossly unfair. For several weeks, I became totally immersed in either feeling sorry for myself or wondering what I needed to do to get my employees to accept me. One night, I was terribly upset. I finally started to ask myself what my feelings were and to try to get to the core reason behind my depression. I realized that I had completely lost control of the situation and was hunkering down for a long battle. I was prepared to be miserable.

"Don't take anything personally."

—Don Miguel Ruiz

I'm feeling really miserable, and complaining about my situation to a friend at work, telling him how unfairly I am being treated. "Some employees are being so cruel to me," I tell him. I explain how worried I am.

He says, "Here you are, finally realizing the desire of your heart, and you are miserable. I am so sorry for you."

His words shock me and really open my eyes. All at once, I realize that I am allowing fear to overwhelm me. But I also realize that I can do something about this and that I can do it now. I see that unless I can somehow regain control of this situation, I will eventually lose my job. At the

same time, I also see that control for me means to control who I am and what I am doing, not to control the people who are against me.

—Virginia, being miserable

My only hope was to do the very best I could, ignore the negativity, and focus on leading others towards our business goals. More than that, I realized that I had to lead with a good attitude. In other words, I had to master the ability NOT TO TAKE IT PERSONALLY.

This was in the midst of one employee's calling my boss and telling him that she was being traumatized by my decision and that she needed therapy for it. And another employee told me that his family had told him that they did not want him working for a pervert.

"Remember: no one can make you feel inferior without your consent."

—Eleanor Roosevelt

The next day, I came in with a better attitude. I still was hurt and scared, but I felt a little better. Each day after that, I did a little better. In some ways, I felt as if I were crawling out of a deep hole, one that had a lid that was pressing down to keep me in. My fear slowly subsided, and my hurt faded. This happened because I was able to forgive the people, as I no longer took their reactions personally. This shift in my attitude did not happen in a single day or a single week, but eventually, I was able to stand without hurt or fear. I became more loving, accepting, and forgiving.

"Fear is not of the present, but only of the past and future."

—A Course in Miracles

The process of walking through the fear during my transition at work resulted in my experiencing a spiritual awakening. I came to realize that without attachment and the fear that accompanies it, there is much more time to look with wonder upon the world and to see people in a new way. Without fear, I almost felt as though I could fly.

Several days before I would make the grand entrance at work dressed as a woman, I asked my friend Robin to help me do a ritual of leaving the masculine tribe and entering the feminine tribe. Robin was a cis-woman (born woman), so she was perfect for the ritual.

> Robin and I begin by lighting a candle that represented the masculine, my male life, the life that I am leaving. I speak about leaving male privilege, leaving behind the privilege that men in our patriarchal society enjoy. I speak of leaving those trappings of masculinity, such as dominance, aggressiveness, judgment, and control. I blow out the candle; I blow out my enrollment in the male tribe.
>
> I light the feminine candle, which represents partnership in decision making, as well as sensitivity, intuition, and nurturing. I speak of finally being able to be honest with the world about who I am. Then I cry out, "I am not who you thought I was!" I feel strongly that my being male was lying about who I am, and now I am being more authentic by coming out as feminine. My intention is to make the gender transition spiritually before I make the physical transition.

—Virginia, Changing Tribes

In retrospect, this ritual was not perfect. I do not consider myself to be a woman; I consider myself as a two-spirit being: someone who has elements of both genders. However, the ritual gave me the confidence and closure to go forward into my new life as Virginia.

On October 29, 2001, I came into work dressed as a woman. I was a little nervous about my choice of clothes, as well as my make-up and overall appearance, but there was no struggle, no fear, no animosity, and no resistance inside myself. I felt nothing but joy and excitement in my accomplishment at making the shift. I had spiritually done the preparatory work months earlier. Despite the real work that I had done to prepare myself and others, some of the reactions that I got from others were not positive. I knew that this negativity was a product of our culture and the ways in which people are inculcated into it. I did not accept anything bad about the personal reactions that were negative. In other words, I did not take those reactions personally.

I now understand what happened then inside me and how it affected my life. Since then, I have felt as though I have walked into a different world: staying in the moment (the NOW) is easier. The world has taken on a magical hue that I find fascinating, and each person seems new and fresh.

This change in my attitude was the result of my battle against fear. What I learned about nonattachment to possessions helped to bring me freedom from fear. I also knew that on some level, my gender travels were a portal to the spiritual, and the fact that I had come home to the feminine opened up something in my spirit that touched a new reality.

Kipling said in one of his poems, "You can meet with triumph and disaster and treat those two imposters just the same." I do not think that he meant for us to be people without passion. Instead, he was speaking of the illusory value of cultural responses to our ego, as these responses have no lasting value. Viewing our world in the reality of nonattachment does indeed make us different. Not taking things personally gives us a clean view of life and more opportunity to love.

My experience in transitioning to female was life-changing, not only externally, but also internally. The transition taught me lessons about life, reality, and the meaning of existence. Once I could release myself from the fetters that I had imposed upon myself in my own mind, the meanings that I had constructed about reality, it became much easier for me not to become ensnared in the meanings about my reality that others had constructed about me. I no longer took those mental constructs of others personally or identified my ego with them, so they no longer had power over me. I was free for the first time in my life. I had completed the initiation.

As I sit and remember the struggle and revelation of those experiences, I am reminded of what Michael Harner[51] said: that one of the reasons a shaman journeys to nonordinary reality is to help others. Since my transition experience, I have been very conscious of the need in my community and world for the understanding of the truths that I learned. Rather than be like the reformed smoker—preaching my newfound truth to whoever would listen, I have waited for the universe to bring persons my way with whom I can share my experiences. My hope is to assist them. One person said to me, "Virginia, I wish I had your freedom, but I don't think I want to change genders to achieve it!" I happily told him that making a gender transition was not necessary, that every one of us has our individual spiritual portal, the opportunity for us to leave ordinary reality to experience nonduality. I told him that his portal was probably not like mine, but that whatever it was, he could step into it, and doing so would be worth it.

Dear reader, what is your portal?

Baptism

Preparation—Buck Speaks

For some time now, I have been preparing myself for the ritual of baptism. Yes, I was baptized when I was a young Baptist, but the

---

51 www.shamanism.org

ritual connected with that part of my past was simply something that many of us did so that we would feel included in our church. As a result, we hoped that we would not have to go to hell when we died.

> I'm dead. I know I'm dead because I'm in that world where I have been told that people go when they die. I see other dead people. All of them have somewhere to go. Some are entering heaven, and others are entering hell. Somehow, I know with great clarity that where they are going is determined by the belief they held when they died. Either they believed that they were saved and were going to heaven, or they believed that they were sinful and unforgiven and were going to hell. Also, I am totally clear that there is no way to get any new information or experience to use in choosing a new or different belief. I am totally stuck and dead, with nowhere to go. Furthermore, time is not moving; I'm really stuck. All I have is the awareness that everyone else is going some-where, while I am going nowhere.[52]

> —Buck dreaming as a child

Not too long after having this dream, I had another dream that I still remember vividly today. I woke up from the dream, still not believing in either heaven or hell. Long after having had this dream, I still have a real problem because I'm without any clear belief about what happens when we die. I fear that I simply won't have any place to go when I die. Maybe this nagging confusion is the root cause of my having been a spiritual seeker since my youth.

Recently, I've been exploring the scriptures on the baptism of Jesus, using Gestalt methodology. I was going through this story,

---

52 One of my childhood dreams.

imagining that I am each character in the allegory and experiencing it from the view of that character. I started doing this one evening after going to bed. It wasn't long before the process evolved into a vivid dream.

In my dream, John the Baptist is a combination of Virginia and the Goddess of Divine Wisdom, Sophia. Sophia speaks to Jehovah to tell him that this ritual symbolizes His being replaced by the God of Love. Jehovah gets angry and expresses His traditional jealous rage. When Sophia tells Him to hand over his tools of power, he opens a drawer in His desk and takes out the keys to the gates of heaven. Then He takes one key at a time and violently throws it into the gate. The keys penetrate the wooden structure as King Arthur's magic sword, Excalibur, was stuck into the rock. Jehovah shouts, "From this time forward, each person entering heaven will have to enter by unlocking the gate for himself."

I realize that the kingdom of heaven and the Garden of Eden are one and the same. Each of us will have to be able to select the right key embedded in the gate, remove the key, and then put it into the lock to open the gate to let ourselves in. From this time forward, there will be no gatekeeper to let us into the Garden of Eden, the kingdom of heaven, other than ourselves. This seems to have answered my childhood question; I'll just use my intuition to select the correct key, open the gate, and let myself in.

Then Sophia asks Him to hand over His magical wand, which he does, but with great reluctance. Sophia passes the wand to an archangel to hold until Jesus is dead and in the grave. Only then can the archangel give the wand to Jesus. He will use it to command the rock that holds him captive within the grave to roll away so that he can leave the tomb.

Still, as Jesus in this dream, I am a candidate for baptism and realize the full responsibility of taking on this ritual and the ensuing tasks. I will have only about three years to accomplish the intermediate tasks before having to proceed with the next ritual—the ritual of death and resurrection. I feel greatly challenged by this realization.

An immediate task will be to select twelve disciples who symbolize twelve aspects of me, each corresponding to a different sign of the zodiac. Every disciple will represent one of my subpersonalities. The task requires identifying the extreme behaviors of each and then defining the balance point or a center point of the polarities, a state that is truly whole and healthy. I am shaken by the understanding that I already am all of these various subpersonalities. Despite realizing this, I really don't know when and how they operate me. Thus I will need to search for twelve followers who will mirror back to me who I am and show me how I am out of balance. My three years of ministry will really be three years of self-study that involves learning how to deal effectively with all their/my dysfunctions.

Other tasks are for me to understand how I'm going to do this, to see whether I'm really motivated for what I've just taken on, and to see whether I believe that I can overcome the challenges that will be presented to me. I exclaim to myself: "Oh, my God, I've got to go alone out into the desert and really consider what I'm going to do!"

Also, I wonder whether I will have to learn how to heal, turn water into wine, make swine crazy, and do other such tasks necessary for the public ministry that lies before me. This I imagine to be especially difficult, given that I won't get the wand of power until after I've finished all of these challenging assignments. Will I have to do all this on my own without any help from Jehovah?

Suddenly, the great dilemma arises in my mind: I really am going to need God's help, but the God I've known is Jehovah, the God of the Old Testament. Yet I also sense that a major part of my task will be to reach the point at which I can say, "Holy Father, I abandon you!"

Gradually, it occurs to me that I have to become entirely the Son of the God of Love instead of the Son of Old God, even though the latter is so innately familiar. After thousands of years in which we humans have been living with the viewpoint of our God as the God of Judgment, Suffering, and Punishments, this will probably take at least three years of intensive practice to change this viewpoint. And I will likely fail at this many times, beginning a speech or lesson initially from the viewpoint of oneness and love, but then lapsing into making a judgment and slipping back into my old mindset of duality. I myself will be taking on the responsibility for making all these slipups, many of which will be recorded in the gospels. My own confusion will, in turn, lead to others' confusion arising from my teachings. This will probably produce repercussions for many generations in the future, including today's generation.

No wonder that it's going to take me forty days of praying and fasting in the desert to plan out all of this after letting my cousin baptize me. I have a lot to deal with that will be even more challenging than the old devil's temptations. "Oh, damn," I think as I realize that I, myself, have actually accepted all of these responsibilities and the consequences of them.

After this dream, I decide to allow my present-day self to have some time to decide whether I really want to undergo this baptism ritual. Unlike Jesus, the candidate of old, I don't want to take on all these ensuing responsibilities without some time to think out their consequences. I'll give myself at least forty days of Gestalt analysis of the baptism allegories, plus many discussions with Virginia, before I can agree to undertake this ritual and the implied subsequent ritual, the ritual of death and resurrection.

Finally, the time arrives for me to undertake the ritual of baptism. No more stalling! I'm going for it.

The Ritual: Buck Continues

Soon after I felt ready to undertake baptism, the oneness trainers began providing Mukhti[53] Deeksha, a blessing ritual designed to initiate an accelerated awakening process. So I scheduled to attend this ritual with Virginia and to get baptized the night before.

We do the baptism ritual in a hot tub in a spa in Santa Fe. Virginia baptizes me. My intention is to proceed with taking up the responsibilities I understand are mine from the preparatory dream. Virginia suggests that I undertake the baptism not only for myself, but also for anyone who is experiencing a similar intention. This I do.

---

53 *Mukhti* is a word used in India to indicate an enlightened person.

Submersion into the water symbolizes my intent to die to my old self, who has been dualist in my viewpoint and in denial of the now obvious fact that I have been being operated by an ego with multiple personalities. Virginia raises me up from the water, and I accept the symbolism of rebirth. Virginia looks into my eyes, and I see Jesus. His presence is a sign to me from the God of Love that He has approved and accepted my intention.

During and after the weekend Mukhti Deeksha process, I realize that the way my mind is viewing and interacting with the world is changing. I feel different, and others notice that I seem different.

I expect that all my spirit guides and teachers are going to be available to help me. But in my first solo mediation after the baptism and the weekend of blessings, I go to the imagined space where I have always gone to encounter my amazing spiritual guides. But all I see are their skeletons. Finally, when I begin to recover from the shock of this vision, I realize that this venture is my own; I have to do it myself.

A teaching of Bhagavan of the Oneness University is to practice the presence of the Divine within. After the vision of my guides as skeletons, I am puzzled as how to practice the presence of the Divine within. But then two or three weeks later, another vision comes to me in my morning meditation. Jesus walks up to me, turns around back to me, and then wisps himself into my heart. I feel him inside me. Then Hiawatha does the same maneuver. I now feel him inside me too. And a few days later, Nanak also does the maneuver. Ever since this incorporation of them into myself, I experience these three as the three wise men and as my sacred friends inside my heart. Now my inner child is surrounded by the three of them.

.

Baptism of Buck—Virginia Speaks

Baptizing Buck was a great adventure and a great honor. He was so filled with the determination to evolve that the process was easy and joyful. Christian baptism is a burial of the old person and a rising out of the water to new life in Jesus. Christian baptism, however, was not the baptism that we experienced. We performed a oneness baptism of our own creation, in which Buck completely released Jehovah, God of Judgment, and accepted and committed his way to the God of Love and oneness. Buck had asked me before the baptism whether I would be the dove in the ritual. In the Biblical story, the dove represents the Holy Spirit and shows up at the moment when Jesus is baptized to show the Father's approval of Jesus and his process. After Buck rose out of the water as the God of Love, I gave Buck Deeksha, a oneness blessing, as we looked into each other's eyes. This moment was intense and powerful. I felt the power and compassion in both of us as we shared the moment when I was the dove energy of the Holy Spirit, approving of Buck's heart and commitment. Buck saw me as Jesus. Our intention was unified.

After the weekend of the baptism and then the Mukhti Deeksha, I saw a change in my dear friend. In what Buck would say and write, I saw that he was looking back at dualism critically, rather than writing and speaking within the dualistic system in an unreflective or an unconscious way. The realization that had happened in his spirit was evident in his new perspective.

Buck Speaks Again

Because of this baptism experience, I feel that I really know Jesus, the candidate for Christ consciousness. Before that event, I had judged the writers of the New Testament as being confused, having Jesus speak with two voices—sometimes as the God of Judgment and sometimes as the God of Love, often in the same Biblical passage. Now I understand that Jesus represents all candidates who have to struggle with deprogramming the subconscious to switch fully from duality to oneness. During this process, which I am currently undergoing, I slip up quite often and make judgments and judgmental statements before I can become aware of what I'm doing. Now I thank the New Testament writers for giving me this deep lesson associated with making such a major transition. It helps me to accept myself.

Also, I can project forward to the follow-up initiation, death and resurrection. I could never understand why Jesus said, just before dying, "My God, My God, why have you forsaken me?"[54] Actually, it is the candidate having the deep realization that he has, at last, completely separated from his old god and is now ready to be resurrected as the God of Love. This is the moment at which Jesus becomes Christ! The ritual of death and resurrection poses a huge challenge. I feel the magnitude of that challenge.

After the Baptism—Buck Speaks

As a result of the processes involved in the ritual of baptism, I've taken on the obligation of getting to know the twelve aspects of my personality. Each aspect corresponds to one of the disciples of Jesus, a sign of the zodiac, and a part of my body. Examining the Apostles behaviors and personalities turns out to be like looking at myself in a mirror. Often by noticing which of Jesus' disciples I'm acting like, I get a more complete picture of myself. This view gives me an opportunity to take some corrective action. Like Peter for example, I can find that I'm stirring up controversy primarily for the purpose of attracting attention to myself; Peter was an attention seeker. I like to rationalize that what I'm doing by bringing up a problem is to be in service to others, but often it is simply to serve my ego.

---

54 Matthew 27:46.

The Apostles and their Astrological Signs

Sign(Date)	Element	Apostle	Body Part
Aries (3/21-4/20	Fire(cardinal)	Peter	head
Taurus (2/21-5/21	Earth(fixed	Simon	neck
Gemini(5/22-6/21)	Air(mutable)	James	arms
Cancer(6/22-7/23)	Water((cardinal)	Andrew	beasts
Leo(7/24-8/23)	Fire(fixed)	John	heart
Virgo(8/24-9/23)	Earth(mutable)	Phillip	bowels
Libra(9/24-10/23)	Air(cardinal)	Nathaniel	kidneys
Scorpio(10/24-11/22)	Water(fixed)	Thomas	genitals
Sagittarus(11/23-12/21)	Fire(mutable)	James	thighs
Capricorn(12/22-1/20)	Earth(cardinal)	Matthew	knees
Aquarius(1/21-2/19)	Air(fixed)	Thaddeus	leg/ankles
Pisces(2/20-3/20)	Water(mutable)	Judas	feet

The first objective is to be able to observe and identify who I am operating as at a given moment. For example, am I behaving as Peter the Aries (cardinal sign of fire), cutting off someone's ear? Or, am I Judas the Pisces (mutable sign of water), feeling so guilty that I want to kill myself? The second objective is to be able to define the balance point of each of the twelve aspects for myself, as well as the behaviors that I have when this part of me is in control.

Buck's Fire Sign Alignments

Aries: Peter (head)

One Extreme   Balance Point   Other Extreme

Impulsive, in denial, likes to save face, needs to learn about karma

Impulsive ==**Discerning** == Afraid to reveal myself
Face-saving ==**Considered Honesty**==Blurting out a "truth"

Leo: John (heart)

Attention-getter, hospitable, loves winning and being loved the best

Getting attention by using controversy == **CarefulNoticing**==Playingblind

Sagittarius: James (thighs)

Loyal, just, and steadfast; fired up with motivation

Unbending ==**Steady & On-Target**==Doesn't give a damn

I began this process by studying the behaviors of the twelve historic disciples of Jesus and their respective astrologic signs. I started with the fire signs: Peter, the Aries (cardinal sign of fire); John, the Leo (fixed sign of fire); and James, the Sagittarius (mutable sign of fire). Next I worked with the earth signs: Matthew, the Capricorn (cardinal sign of earth); Simon, the Taurus (fixed sign of earth); and Phillip, the Virgo (mutable sign of earth). Then I worked with the apostles who represent the water signs are: Andrew, the Cancer (cardinal sign of water); Thomas, the Scorpio (fixed sign of water); and Judas, the Pisces (mutable sign of water). Finally, the air signs are represented by: Nathaniel, the Libra (cardinal sign of air); Thaddeus, the Aquarius (fixed sign of air); and James, the Gemini (mutable sign of air). The results for my element of fire are shown above. You, when you do this, will probably have somewhat different results. For example, I can be out of balance in either of two directions. As Peter, who balance point for me of **Being Discerning** and **Considered**

Honesty can be for example, on the one hand, **Face-Saving and maybe even lying**, and on the other hand, **Blurting Out the Truth**. The chart above shows what I've found out about my fire signs.

The tools I'm using to get a deeper understanding of how these twelve subpersonalities operate in me are self-awareness, meditation and yoga. Setting a clear intention to use this method to increase my self understanding is a key part of the process. Also it is proving helpful to do this practice with companions; for me this is with Virginia or Gurubhai. The yoga is the technique of standing still, breathing deeply, and giving attention to parts of the body as a source of deep and often hidden aspects of self.[55] Since each disciple is associated with a part of the body, focusing into this body part can be revealing. For example, the throat is the location of Simon the Taurus and the place where we speak truth, hide truth, or lie. It is also the place where we can recognize getting stiff necked and bull headed about something. In other words, the body can have a primary role in this process of becoming self-aware. We've also learned that associating each subpersonality with an area of the body helps me remember the subpersonalities and their qualities.

When the balance point of a specific subpersonality is found and expressed powerfully, it seems to provide higher spiritual powers. For example, Peter can present as competent spiritual leadership, John as unconditional love, and James as Divine Will and action. When fire and water are in balance, metabolism becomes balanced, and I feel healthier and more energetic.

In summary, each disciple with their corresponding astrological sign represents a dimension of my personality. My ego, together with prior programming, keeps me unconsciously under their spells and tips me away from their respective balance points. Awareness of which subpersonality is in control at a given moment helps me locate my behavior on their individual scales. For example, as John, the archetype of unconditional love, I can ask myself as I when I find I am under his influence: "Am I under-doing John by being too reserved with my love; or am I balanced John by expressing an appropriate amount of love; or am I overdoing John and becoming

---

55 Stephen Cole; *Yoga and the Quest for the True Self* (New York, NY: Bantam Press, 1999), p. 229.

obsequious. Knowing this then gives me the opportunity to decide if this is really what I want to be doing just now or if I want to change something. The answer to this question often comes as I bring my attention to the appropriate body part, in this case to my heart. I can thus use the subpersonality to my advantage rather than having the subpersonality unconsciously use me. As I become more aware of all twelve aspects of myself, it is easier to bring them into balance, and thus I become freer of ego control and eventually more spontaneous.

Conclusion

The ritual of baptism seems be a prelude to the death and resurrection ritual. It is a rising out of the waters to accept the opportunity to become new. It indicates an intention and a willingness to allow the dualistic viewpoint to die, to empty oneself of duality. And it is also seen as a commitment to do the work, not only of emptying, but also of balancing so that we can be ready to be filled with a oneness view of our selves and our world—ready to be filled with the Divine—ready for awakening into Christ consciousness. As Nathaniel says to Jesus, "Dying is like walking from one room into the next."[56] When we die, we don't have to imagine a heaven because we will already be in heaven, the heaven on earth obtained by living life filled with the joy of the internalized divine, just as Jesus, the Son of the God of Love, promised us.

The Sermon on the Mount

Virginia Speaks

Blessed are the pure in heart, for they shall see God[57].

—*Jesus*

_____

56 See The Last Supper, Part 2 (below).
57 Matthew 5:8

When Buck and I got to the fifth chapter of the Gospel According to Matthew, I was very excited because from our work so far, I felt that I could interpret any and all stories in the Bible with the experiential process that we had been using. But the Sermon on the Mount[58] posed some new challenges. The text is full of comforting and uplifting passages, for example:

5:5   Blessed are the meek, for they shall inherit the Earth.
5:14   You are the Light of the world.
5:44   Love your enemies and pray for those who persecute you.
6:21   Where your treasure is, there will your heart be also.
6:25   Do not worry about your life, what you will eat or drink.

—Jesus

However, it is also filled with harsh or judgmental language, for example:

5:17   Do not think that I have come to abolish the law or the prophets. I have not come to abolish them, but to fulfill them.
5:19   Anyone who breaks one of the least of these commandments and teaches others to do the same will be called least in the kingdom of heaven.

—Jesus

Therefore, I set my heart to look at the allegorical meaning and not to labor over the literal meaning of the verses. In the end, this allegory became an initiation for both of us.

As I read the Sermon on the Mount, I think about Buck, his pilgrimages to the Oneness University, and his being a provider of oneness blessings. I think about how wonderful he is at blessing others and how grateful I am for having him in my life. As

58 Matthew 5–7

I read the first twelve verses of Matthew, chapter five, I find that the text addresses those who are blessed. In my spirit, I know that the message for me is to bless others. It is my nature and Buck's nature to bless others. In looking at the totality of Matthew, chapters five through seven, rather than at the individual verses, I see that the allegorical interpretation is exactly this. I also recognize that the next time I read this chapter, it might say something to me completely new! But for today, it says that I am to bless, just as Jesus blessed. So I write out the words that come to me.

As I read what I have written, I feel richly blessed, and I feel that the message has become part of me. So when next Buck and I meet, it feels so natural and right for me to take Buck's hands, look into his eyes, and say that this is a message from Jesus to Buck. As I speak the words, I know that I spiritually dwell in the God position.

This is what I say to him:

> You are blessed when you are **humble**, when you mourn for what you have loved and lost, when you thirst for the ascendancy of your magical child, when you have patience, when you show mercy, when you demonstrate integrity, when you make peace with yourself and others, when you absorb false criticism, and when you are persecuted unjustly. You are blessed when your heart is here.
>
> As you are blessed, go and bless others.
>
> Your blessings on others shall not be in taking credit, showing your goodness, or making money. ***Your blessings are pure, as your heart is pure.***
>
> What you do comes from your heart. If you bless others, as I do, then in your heart are joys, love, peace, and compassion. You are giving my heart as you bless.

As you bless, you do not have the time, the nature, or the desire to blame others, to be disloyal, to feel sorry for yourself, or to strike back if attacked, either by word or by hand. *But it is now your nature and desire only to give others love, joy, and peace.* If someone does you wrong or criticizes you, that just means that they need more of your blessing.

Be ready to give what you have to those who do not have, for in doing this, you bless them, and it is your nature to do so. For in doing this, your cup will be filled. It is indeed more blessed to give than to receive.

Even so, receive the blessing from others with deep humility and gratitude, knowing that it is not the vessel that blesses, but it is the living water that pours from me to you through willing vessels that blesses you.

As you bless others, your spirit, body, and soul shall be transfigured, your heart shall be golden, and your eye shall be full of light. All the more reason to bow before the child, the beggar, or the king in the humility within you.

Therefore I tell you to lose all of your fears about being poor, being hungry, or not having friends, about dying or getting sick, and do not consider your reputation even something to grasp. Instead, trust in your magical child and then in me with you to provide for all of your needs. It is your nature now to walk through the world without fear. If you have no fear and but trust your way, then you will not worry.

But place your intention on being a blessing and in blessing others, and your life shall be without want, fear, or worry.

> **Consider that you have in you a precious pearl, so precious that people would sell all that they possess to get it. Now with all your intention, give that never-ending pearl away to all whom you can. Believe that you are giving them me and you.**
>
> — Virginia as Jesus

After I speak as Jesus these words to Buck, we both are crying. I know that not only are the words the expression of the Divine for us, but that Buck has been blessed by the words and that I have been greatly blessed as well. Believe me, those double blessings are very enjoyable! All of our appointments with people can be this way. We move with compassion and speak or minister to the people we meet and with whom we interact. They come away blessed, and so do we. When I walk out of my house in the morning, I have the intention to have a divine appointment with someone that day. It may be a clerk at the supermarket, a homeless man begging for beer money, a politician looking for my vote, or a friend I just happen to run into. But I shall be able to bless that person that day with a kind word, a bit of money, a healing word, a prophecy, or a word of wisdom. I walk away deeply blessed as well. By experiencing the Sermon on the Mount internally, I realize again that our process enables us to see the meaning of the story and have it live within us. There is no need to memorize it and no need to hear a sermon. The nature to bless is mine, and it is an intrinsic part of me.

The Sermon on the Mount—Buck's Comments

Virginia takes my hands to tell me to look directly into her eyes. She is Virginia, and she is Jesus. For the first time in my life, I am able to hear and understand the Sermon on the Mount. Tears roll down my cheeks! I understand, and my heart flowers.

At the Oneness University, I heard about the flowering of the heart, but now, I am actually having this experience. It is Virginia/Jesus who actually gives me my final initiation as a giver of blessings.

The Last Supper: Part I: The Conflict

The Story: And as they were eating, Jesus took bread, blessed it, broke it, gave it to the disciples, and said, "Take. Eat. This is my body."

And he took the cup, gave thanks, and gave it to them, saying, "Drink ye all of it: for this is my blood of the new testament, which is shed for many for the remission of sins. But I say unto you, I will not drink henceforth of this fruit of the vine until that day when I drink it new with you in my Father's kingdom.[59]

We reenact this, using the Gestalt process. We sit at a large table, with a beautiful tablecloth, a cup with wine, a plate with a piece of bread, and a bowl.

We examined this allegory, by actually doing the last supper ritual and then we told each other our experiences as we took on different roles of the different participants in the feast.

Jesus

How I love all the people gathered here: Mary, Mary Magdalene, Peter, John, plus all the other women and disciples present. Nevertheless, as I face my impending death and resurrection ritual, I desperately fear that they have not understood the message that I tried to teach them. They have seen the miracles that a heart of love and compassion can accomplish. They have believed the miracles and have listened to my teachings. But they still fail to see how my words apply to them. Instead of internalizing my words and seeing a new world within themselves,

---

59 Matthew 26:26–29

they insist on worshipping me and seeing me as something special, as God-made-flesh. After the ritual, this will be further reinforced as I assume the position of the God of Love.

John almost has it because of our relationship, and Mary Magdalene almost gets it too. But every person must come to the realization on his or her own: each person is God. That is why I taught in parables, stories, and actions—because I wanted them to get it for themselves that they could do all the things that I have done—and even greater things—because of their unity with each other. I have been a pattern for them to show them the way. They can follow my example and enter the kingdom. I pray that they will.

As I pick up the bread, I am so filled with love for them all that I cry. As I tell them to eat of my body, I am trying to impart to them the fact that we are one, that there is no difference between them and me or them and each other. Adam and Eve knew this in the Garden of Eden, and I have been sent to show the way back there. As I give them the wine, I am still crying and tell them to drink of my blood. This is a further statement on nonduality and the oneness of all people.

Have I failed? Will they not see this oneness? Will they continue to worship me, granting me a unique status in all of Creation? Will my ministry be in vain as they continue not to internalize my teaching and not to realize the oneness of all?

I must keep trying right up until the end. I am concerned that I have failed in my life's purpose to show them the way to my Father, to the place where we are one.

—Virginia as Jesus

Judas

I have a deep longing to be recognized by the Master as a special companion, as the special person that I am. "After all," I say almost out loud, "am I not the most educated and intelligent?" I've always longed for Jesus to kiss me as he kisses John; he mostly ignores me. "It just doesn't make sense that he should love John the most, especially when John is so often out of control."

—Buck as Judas before the supper

I am very cool and careful. My behavior is apparently innocent and unsuspecting. Silently, I go over my rationalization that I haven't gotten any benefit from spending all these years serving Jesus. I feel justified in doing what I am doing. It is a way for me to get paid for my years of service. I continue to dine and talk. My participation is appropriate, automatic, and without any expression of my well-hidden feelings or plans.

—Buck as Judas after the supper

The turning point comes after I return with the temple guards. They are watching as I kiss Jesus. When my lips touch his face, they start to burn, and I want to cry out, as I am awakened in this instant to a full realization of what I am doing. Still hiding my feelings, I quickly leave, feeling invaded by madness, an increasing madness that overtakes me. I am trying to escape from myself and from whom I have just discovered myself to be. Suicide is my only escape from this horrible existence as I finally become fully aware of what I have done. I am relieved not to have to breathe even one more time.

—Buck as Judas with the guards

John [*Note to reader. See footnote before reading*[60]]

> *Then Peter, turning about, seeth the disciple whom Jesus loved following who also leaned on his breast at supper, and said, "Lord, which is he that betrayeth thee?"*[61]

I love that man! I worship him. He is incredibly kind and gentle, but at the same time filled with a power built upon his self-confidence and oneness of purpose. Being with him has changed me. All this talk of his death is very depressing, and I cannot consider it, or I dissolve into tears. I am changed because of his love for me.

Loving him has been the greatest experience of my life. The feel of his body, the warmth of his embrace, the power of his whispers in intimacy, all have brought me to a pinnacle of love. But I know that he will never be mine. He is too big for that. The love he has for all people is the love

---

60 Note to the reader: this channeling includes a graphic description of love-making between John and Jesus. It is not our wish to offend anyone, but we felt it was important to include this because of our culture's reluctance to find union and even intersection between sexuality and spirituality. The suggestion that Jesus never had sex supports the idea that sexuality and sacred things are to be separate, yet we feel very strongly that the two can be, and are, one.

61 John 21:20.

of his life, yet I feel privileged to have glimpsed love through our relationship. Even though we shared our love with intimacy, he never treated me differently than the others. He never favored me. He treated all the same because he loved us all.

Our special events of lovemaking gave me a look into another world. As I experienced his body, I felt so much larger than myself. I felt like a participant in the whole world. When he would caress me with his lips, tasting me, and then move to even more passionate love, I felt as if I were experiencing the love of the whole world.

When I would return his caresses and tasted him, I felt as if I were receiving the most precious gift in the world, that I was participating in His loving all the people in the world. Those were truly the most special moments I have ever experienced.

When we made love, I somehow felt like his teachings were being imparted to me through the process of love. He also taught me how to experience his love when he was not around: to consider all people neither better nor greater than myself, but to love them as I love myself and to treat them as I would wish to be treated. I love him with all of my being. He would say to that, "John, love all people just as you have loved me."

—Virginia speaks as John

Peter

I feel great pride just sitting on the right hand of the Master, and I feel assured that this will be my position forever. The Passover supper is for me a great joy. I place my hand on my sword and feel reassured—safe and secure. I know that I am ready to protect my lord and master if need be.

Looking back, I can see that I was in great denial of what was about to happen. The great wine, delicious food, and wonderful companionship were the focus of my feeling as I sat there next to my beloved Jesus.

After the supper, we go outside with Jesus. He wants to pray, and we are instructed by Him to stay close, yet to give him some private space so that he can pray without interruption or distraction.

Suddenly, He is shaking me, waking me up, and He is annoyed that the others and I are asleep. But when he returns to his prayers, I, with my wine-soaked brain, simply fall back into sleep. Suddenly, I am again awakened; this time by the rustling noises of movement. Startled, I see a crowd of people, including Judas, who kisses Jesus. From the way Judas behaves after the kiss, I know that something is going wrong, seriously wrong. Some in the crowd grab and bind Jesus. They arrest him and started to lead him away. Flushed with anger, I draw my sword. Swinging it wildly, I cut off the ear of one of the guards. I catch the eye of Jesus; his look tells me to desist. My anger turns to shame, and I just don't know what to feel anymore.

I follow somewhat behind the crowd of men who are leading Jesus away. Later, I arrive at the place where they are questioning him. I feel estranged from Jesus and from all that is happening. Someone asks me, "Aren't you a member of His party?" An immediate "No" comes out of my mouth, followed by: "I don't know him." This scene is repeated two more times. Then I hear a cock crow, and I come to my senses. I back away, realizing the Jesus really knows me much better than I know myself. He really is the Master.

—Buck as Peter

Jesus, Not at the Supper, but from the previous Baptism Ritual

I am telling my story of the Last Supper to John the Baptist. I confess to John that I haven't succeeded in bringing my twelve subpersonalities into balance as I remember the behaviors of my inner John, Peter, and Judas during the Last Supper. I am fully aware of the importance of having to go through the death and resurrection ritual to shed finally my attachment to the Old Testament God. I am truly ready to become the Son of the God of Love, the New Testament God. As I break the bread, symbolizing my body, and feed it to all of my subparts, this is a sign to them that they too will have to undergo this same transition. As I give them the fruit of the vine to drink, it is the pouring out of the last drops of my blood, the blood of devotion to the old god. I know that they too, in time, will also have to have this experience. And when they do, we will become one—whole and balanced. Only then can we truly celebrate my real victory by sharing the fruit of the vine.

—Buck as Jesus

Buck Confesses

This ritual strongly reminds me of the incompleteness of my journey, of how I really haven't gotten to know fully my inner family of subpersonalities. Furthermore, it is only since the baptism ritual that I've started to become aware of them and notice how I allow them to control me.

I expected to undertake the death and resurrection ritual some time in the future, probably after I finished writing this book. Now with this Last Supper ritual, I realize how unready I am for this. I also realize how motivated I am to get ready. I only know six of the twelve disciples, but am now just becoming aware of how they are influencing my thoughts and behaviors. Perhaps the easiest one to identify with is Peter, the Aries, who takes immediate action without considering the consequences. The hardest one, so far, is John the Leo, who personifies that part of self so capable of unconditional love. However, when I am giving oneness blessings, I am definitely practicing unconditional love. I am also beginning to be able to identify with the emotional state of Judas the Pisces within myself.

I feel ready to surrender my attachment to the Old Testament God of Judgment and Punishment, yet almost daily, I catch myself slipping back into this automatic behavior of judging others and myself. Definitely, I need more practice to fully exercise this intention automatically.

140

The Last Supper: Part 2: The Resolution

The Story: *The written text for this story is already familiar: the text of the canonical gospels themselves. What is unfamiliar, perhaps, is the point of view: it comes from one of us (Buck) participating in a ritual led by Hunter Flournoy, a mystic and healer in the Eastern Christian tradition. Hunter explained a radically different vision of the Last Supper. In his own words:*

"When Jesus took the bread, gave it to his friends, and said, 'do this in remembrance of me,' it was in the same spirit as his invitations to love one another as he loved us; not sharing his body with each other, but sharing our own bodies with each other, and thus becoming one with him in the act of giving ourselves and receiving each other completely. As Jesus said, 'There is no greater love than this, that we give our lives to each other;' and so, with Jesus, we say, 'This is my own body, my own blood, and I give them to you, that we may be One, as I and my father, my mother, the source of my being, are One.' Furthermore, Jesus insisted that we receive not only the spiritual body (soma), but the physical body (sarx) of each other as well – the scent, vibration, touch, taste, and vision of our animal bodies as holy and wholly delightful incarnations of divine oneness – experienced innocently, with all the pleasure and joy of an infant discovering its own marvelous sensuality for the first time. Behold, in the communion of Love we make all things new!"

–Hunter Flournoy, The Erotic Body of Christ

141

This ritual takes place several months after the first one. The setting is in a motel room in Truth or Consequences, New Mexico. The room is equipped with a large tub that can be filled with the natural hot spring waters of this region. These are sacred waters that have been used continually for healing since long before Europeans arrived in the New World.

We begin our ritual by setting up a sacred space and invoking the archangels to protect and aid us. We do the ritual while sitting in the warm healing water. After a prayer of thanksgiving, we apply to each other the scent of spikenard to invoke in divine feminine, the scent of frankincense to invoke the divine masculine, and the scent of lavender (with a hint of both spikenard and frankincense) to invoke the divine child.

We share the bread, looking into each other's eyes and saying words in the nature of: "This is my body, take and eat, and become one with me." We share the wine, still looking in each other's eyes and saying something like: "This is my blood, my life force; drink, and become one with me." Our eyes are flooded with tears from the deep, deep feelings of love and oneness that arise in us.

The ritual continues as we become our infant selves and start making our first recognized self-aware sounds. Soon, we are laughing uproariously.

We then share touch. This starts with foot washing, the usual version of the ritual. But in this ritual, we actually bathe each other, starting, of course, with the feet, which symbolize Judas. Virginia, now as Jesus, points out to Judas that he must surrender his thinking mode of being in the world to understand what is really going on. "No way," thinks Judas, who is in denial of his feelings.

This process continues, with the role of Jesus switching spontaneously back and forth between the two of us. The washing follows the order of signs of the zodiac, where Judas is the twelfth sign, Pisces, and Peter is the first sign, Aries. Thus the bathing moves slowly from the feet to the face, through the twelve areas of the body, each of which represents one of the disciples.

As this happens, the teachings begin to flow in both directions. Jesus is suddenly recognizing the essential teachings that he has been receiving from each of the disciples. He is realizing that each has been and still is a mirror of himself, that his self-understanding was made available to him by observing and interacting with his companions. He is awakening with great wonder to the fact that they have been his teachers all this time. His self-awareness is unfolding as the washing goes from one disciple to the next. He understands that his assumption that he was their teacher had been blinding him to knowing their true roles in his life. He explains, "My companions, my friends, my mirrors, my teachers, with this ritual, you are allowing me to be readied for my final ritual. When we finished eating, I was in judgment of both myself and of you. But now, as we bathed each other, we are allowing ourselves to surrender completely to our mutual love; and, in this state of oneness with all of you, I am now humble enough and sufficiently prepared to move to the end."

Virginia Speaks

In Part I, we experienced the worry and fear that Jesus had that the disciples and the women with him had not understood his message of oneness and that his ministry had been in vain. In Part 2, we experienced the resolution of the predicament in which Jesus thought that his mission had failed.

Buck and I were sharing our bread and wine with each other. Buck began to speak as Jesus and told a beautiful and complete summary. Just as we were sharing each other's body and blood, we were one with each other and, by spiritual extension, one with all things. The issue was not whether Jesus was divine. The mission of Jesus had been to show people the way and the pattern to obtain God consciousness and God realization through their spiritual experience. I came to realize that the disciples and the women had understood this at the Last Supper.

Nathaniel

Jesus, now we understand. I did not see it before. I felt as though I had no right to claim

143

that God was inside me, that somehow that would have been overreaching my worthiness and ability. But now I see it. Now I understand that you have been teaching and showing us the way to find the God within and then to be able to move with the power of compassion and love to bless our world and all the multitudes. Now I also see something else. I see that death truly has no power over us, that our existence will ever be and shall never burn out. Death is just another transition. It is like moving from one room to another. Oh, sure—we will miss terribly the people we love when they die, but death will never be the ultimate victor over us. Your teachings have set me free from the law of sin and death.

—Virginia channels Nathaniel

Virginia Reflects

I, as Nathaniel, said those words to Buck as he was Jesus. All at once, Buck realized that Nathaniel was teaching Jesus because he was facing his ritual of death and resurrection. He was worried and fearful about that ritual. Could he do it? Hearing the words of Nathaniel set Jesus free from his fear of death and enabled him to look toward the ritual as his final statement of oneness. This further exemplified the interaction of experience and learning that took place between Jesus and the disciples, as well as between Jesus and the women who followed him during the years of his ministry. The crowning realization was that the disciples had indeed understood his message and his mission. The problem of Part I was resolved, and now Jesus was set for the ritual of death and resurrection.

Buck Reflects

Being Jesus during the washing of the bodies of the disciples and their washing my body, I have many realizations. The washing itself removes all barriers that I had set up between my disciples and me. I was no longer top dog; I was their equal. Unlike avatars of the past, I was unique in that each of my followers was a mirror of myself, and now that the mirrors were washed clean, I could see them for who they truly were and how they reflected back to me who I truly was. I needed them as much as they needed me. At last I could fully appreciate that each reflected back to me a unique subpersonality. Only through all of them could I truly see my whole self. This washing experience completely changed the way I viewed the world. When the washing ceremony was over, I was finally ready for the next step in my journey to become the Son of the God of Love. My disciples have successfully washed away all my judgments of them and of myself.

Buck Speaks after the Ceremony

When the ritual is complete and we have thanked and dismissed the archangels, we lie on the bed. Our bodies are warm from being in the hot water so long, but now the cool air of the air conditioner is blowing across us. I recall that we had discussed that this ritual might become sexual. But what actually happened seemed so much more powerful than any sexual experience. I remember that as I was Jesus bathing Virginia and came to the genital area, I was experiencing bathing Thomas, the Scorpio, who corresponds to this region of the body. I was healing him from his fears, his doubts, his jealousies, and his uncertainties. I loved him for the whole of who he was with all of his hesitancy and self-doubt. There was no sexual arousal, but there was the deepest affection, appreciation, and respect.

At another point during this period of lying in bed, with drifting awareness and minimal conversation, I remember Virginia saying to me: "You are in the God position." I slowly examine this idea, and my mind drifts to the bit I wrote just before leaving for this adventure. It was about my experience in India where we relived, with full emotion, the experiences in which we didn't love ourselves, where we were ashamed, guilty, and felt sinful, but at the end of the experience, we were forgiving and loved ourselves.[62] I drift further into a very expansive state of consciousness, in which I am the Creator, fully experiencing everything that I have ever created: famine, pestilence, births and deaths, plantings and harvests—all the sorrows, all the joys, all the horrors, and all the beauty. I feel great compassion for myself. I am God feeling compassion for myself. I experience everything through all time and Creation as one Self. I love the whole of my God-Self and realize that this is necessary for me to understand my Godhood. For the first time in my life, I really experience the God position. At last, I understand Virginia's experience of this state.

To love is to accept yourself as you are.

—*Bhagavan*

A Sequel to this Ceremony

Nine days after this ceremony of bathing and cleansing, I awaken after having a dream about human spirits tormenting each other in very gross ways. As I set to do my usual morning meditation, I can't get the miserable images from this dream to disappear from my inner vision. I ask my guides to help clear my mind by giving me Deeksha (oneness blessings). This does the job.

Suddenly Bhagavan[63] appears. He busies himself unfolding a tablecloth and takes out some

---

62 "Anything experienced fully, turns to joy." Bhagavan

63 Bhagavan is the living founder of the Oneness Movement, the Oneness University and Temple in India.

bread, slices it, and then proceeds to offer it to my guides, one at a time. He says to Jesus: "This is my body. Take, eat, and become one with me." Jesus gratefully takes the bread and eats.

Then he says to Nanak: "This is my body. Take, eat, and become one with me." Nanak gratefully takes the bread and eats.

Then he says to Hiawatha: "This is my body. Take, eat and become one with me." Hiawatha gratefully takes the bread and eats.

Next he turns to my inner child, who is always sitting between these three great teachers (his three wise men), and Bhagavan says to my inner child: "This is my body. Take, eat, and become one with me." Somewhat surprised, my inner child does take and eat.

Then he addresses me directly, saying: "This is my body. Take, eat, and become one with me." I am totally overwhelmed with gratitude. I accept his gift and eat.

Bhagavan repeats this process with some wine, saying to each of us in turn, "This is my blood, my life force, my essence. Take, drink, and become one with me." Gratefully, each of us accepts this gift. This is followed by simple prayers of thanksgiving.

Now I understand this as the oneness communion and as by far the most powerful blessing that I have ever experienced. Every time I recall this, tears of divine joy flow from my eyes.

—Buck's visualization during meditation

A new Spiritual Practice

With this experience, this Gnostic form of the Last Supper, now becomes a way to celebrate our feelings of oneness with others.

The Crucifixion

We have not undertaken the crucifixion of Jesus as our last initiation, rather Virginia chose a ritual from the ancient Babylonians. This initiation will be presented in the next section. Buck hasn't chosen his yet. What we did however, was to allow ourselves to envision and experience Jesus prior to the crucifixion and as the cross upon which Jesus was nailed. Here is what we experienced.

Jesus' Final Thoughts about Judas

The world is a mirror. The situations you experience in the world outside are a reflection of your inner state of consciousness.

—*Bhagavan*

All these people are trying to get me into arguing with them, I hear their words, their angry accusations and judgments, as well as their hatred and confusion. I know that the public is also angry because they are still under Roman domination and the Romans are aware that the Jews are in a rebelious mood and don't want them to rebel. I know that I'm the scapegoat but this is not my concern. Rather my mind is in deep contemplation of what Judas has mirrored back to me. He allowed me to witness my self-judgment and well as the judgments I was making about all the disciples. It is Judas and his suicide that keeps reemerging in my awareness. I am now in the midst my own suffering and pending death.But I also realize that something much bigger is happening. I do not know that I am worthy to do this ritual. What really is dying is the last residuals of attachment to my old God and to the dualistic view of the world that he symbolizes. I am pregnant with a complete vision of a new God. This body will be gone, but this child will not. What I will leave behind is the possibility that this child will exist within all who come after me. I am praying that they will be able to learn in a much easier way that I've had to learn. I am also giving thanks that this pathway has actually been my pathway to becoming Christ. And I am also praying that others will follow me on this path and that it will be easier for them. When I realize that I will be resurrected as the innocent child of the God of Love, my feeling of worth returns. And I am blessing everyone with this new love.

—Buck as Jesus during his trial

If you recognize that divine grace flows into your life as coincidences, you rise in love and gratitude.

—Bhagavan

The Cross

I'm standing here on this hill, centered between two other crosses. I feel so disgusted that this hanging is my last task on this earth. To ease my pain, I think back to when I had real roots wandering around in the ground and leaves moving in the breezes. I could sing then, and I could host birds that also loved to sing, as I did. I made shade; how lovely it was to give my shade to young lovers, along with the love songs provided by my leaves and the birds.

Now, if I had eyes like those animals that cut me down and raised me up again so they could torment and kill one of their own on my barren and silent structure, I would cry.[64]

Buck as the Cross

Once I was a tall and stately cedar tree, with roots deep in the earth and wide branches to enjoy the sun, the wind, and the rain. But now the Romans have cut me down and have made me into an instrument of torture and death. This is not my nature. This is against my will.

After being carried and dragged through the city, I am laid down on the hill. Now they will nail some poor person to me, and we shall be elevated before all to see his suffering and my shame.

As the first nail is driven through him and into me, I immediately sense something different than before. The others who were nailed on me had different blood. The blood of this man is distinctive. I feel the blood flowing through the porousness of my wood, and I can feel my shame fading away. Who is this man?

---

64 Independently, we each experience the Cross. First two paragraphs written by Buck, the last four paragraphs written by Virginia.

As the other two nails are driven into me, I feel again a kind of freedom and a kind of joy that I have not felt since I was whole and standing tall upon the shores of Galilee. Somehow, I feel a connection with this man. I feel that he is aware of me! This has never happened before. As I stand there on the hill, with this man's blood flowing into me, I feel again my roots, going deep into the earth. I feel again the wind, the rain, and the sun. I feel again my purpose on the earth. If this man has to die on me, I wish for him to die as gently and as quickly as possible. He has set me free from my shame.

Virginia as the Cross

Death and Resurrection

Virginia's Ritual

Ritual Preparation—Virginia Speaks

I decided to use the Inanna myth (see appendices) for my initiation into death and resurrection. Even though I used a non-Biblical myth for my death and resurrection experience, the process of preparing for the ritual gave me great insight into the mystery of the Biblical story of Christ's Crucifixion and Resurrection.

I wrote my own death and rebirth ritual. I did the ritual with the intention of internalizing the truths into the deep space of my heart and, indeed, for a wider community as a whole. I had been deeply troubled for years at the oppression, inequality, and violence suffered by my beloved transgender community. I wrote the ritual as a spiritual vehicle so that we could be transformed from that place of oppression to a state in which we could receive peace and victory in our lives. As my guides and elders led me through the preparation for the ritual, it became apparent that although one intention was for the community, my connection to the ritual had to be my heart space. It became clear that I had to allow myself to be transformed through the ceremony. Jesus might well have felt the same thing according to this pericope in Philippians.[65]

Your attitude should be the same as that of Christ Jesus, who, being in very nature God, did not consider equality with God something to be grasped, but made himself nothing, taking the very nature of a servant, being made in human likeness. And being found in appearance as a man, he humbled himself and became obedient to death—even death on a cross! Therefore God exalted him to the highest place and gave him the name that is above every name.

The Ritual—Virginia Speaks

My ritual was held underground, in a kiva (a circular ritual chamber originally used for Native American ceremonies). I was attended by my five closest spiritual friends, including Buck. I had to give up everything during the passage through the seven gates to hell. The seven things common to the trans-community that I confronted and let go were:
cultural scorn and ridicule,
patriarchal oppression,
family separations,
loss of social status,
feelings of being unsafe in certain situations,
legal discrimination, and
control over my life.

As I step up to the third gate, I hear the words that Wren is speaking,

"This pin represents your third offering. It represents your familial grounding. Challenging

---

65 Philippians 2:5-9 (periscope is quotation for the Bible often read during some Catholic servies.)

gender roles often means losing the good standing that we enjoy in our families. Becoming our trans-selves often means risking the security and support that comes from following familial norms. For many of us, it means losing our marriage and the closeness of our children."

I hear these words and step into the circle to walk around it, but all of a sudden, I am struck by a greater sadness, pain, and suffering than I had ever felt before. It is as if every mother, father, child, or parent who has ever suffered in this way was crying out in pain, and I feel it all. I cry uncontrollably, and Leeza leads me around the circle, as I am blind from the tears. As I reach the altar, I place the pin on the altar, meaning that I give up that pain and suffering and surrender it to the universe. It is no longer mine, but I shall never forget that I carried it.

—Virginia as the initiate

As I approached each gate, I was challenged to give up a part of my attire. Each garment was symbolic of something important in my life. I came through the seventh gate totally nude. As I walked the circles for each of these things, I could feel the weight of the misery that many of us have had to endure in our gender journeys. As I cried with the intensity of these feelings, I was also able to give them up to the altar and release them for myself and my community. In this way, I lost my attachment to the suffering.

The second part was a representative burial. As I lay still under blankets, the elders talked of my life as though I were dead. Then they gently awakened me with care to experience the new birth. I then drank the water of life and entered the resurrection part of the ritual.

The God Position—Virginia Speaks

In the days following the ritual, I was able to say: "Am I in the nature of God? Most definitely! God lives within me and within you. I do not consider the God-nature something to be grasped; I consider it an intrinsic part of my nature.

I realized that I had been a servant to my community and that I had humbled myself and borne the sorrows and suffering on my back that day. I had died, but now lived again. My experience paralleled the experience of Jesus as a bodhisattva. It also paralleled the myth of the crucifixion and resurrection. But I also realized that I had been changed to realize that I was God—not the God of the Bible, but the Christ consciousness available to us all. In this God position, I now know what forgiveness means when Jesus said forgive others seventy times seven times. I can bless others, and I can heal and pray for people's joy and wisdom.

In my journal, I wrote what I had spoken during the resurrection part of the ritual:

> Rebirth raises me to new life. In ancient texts, God's glory filled the temple, and those there felt it and recognized the glory of God as something deep that touched their nature. When I walk into a room, my glory fills the room, and my glory can bless many people. I am no longer subject to the old ways of thinking, where our glory has been stripped from us by a prejudiced culture. My light will shine and be a blessing to all. The days of trans-people being held in lesser regard and looked down upon are over and offered on the altar. We hold the ancient places to usher in a new day for the world. We hold compassion for the world's enlightenment. Power comes by one word: **compassion**. First,

this means to have compassion for myself and to go deeply within and love myself enough to know myself. Second, it means to have compassion for others—to love and to heal where there is sickness, to bring wisdom where there is uncertainty, hope where there is despair, and joy where there is sorrow. My power changes me, making me able to change my world. I am worthy of these things."

—Virginia journaling

As I spoke those words in ritual space, I realized that I had known that God was within me, but I had not assumed the **position** of God being within me. Now I knew that this was who I am. To explain further, I am not the dualistic God of the Bible; I am the God who is all and who is in all. I am the Christ consciousness that is available to us all. Furthermore, I saw that my trans-community had also been raised with me to new life and that a wonderful beginning of transformation has occurred in the trans-community. It was as if the ritual had broken the bondage in another dimension. In this dimension, we will see the freedom of the ritual change people's lives. We are beautiful people. We can hold our heads high. We are a spiritual people. We can facilitate healing. We are a wise people. We can bring mediation and counsel. We are a compassionate people, and we can love.

Since the ritual, I have looked upon the world with new eyes. I know the sorrow and suffering of the world, but I am not subject to it any longer because I have given up my attachment to the suffering. The supposed limits in my life I look upon as impermanent. I can do anything and be what I am called to be. My holiness envelops the whole world, and my love can change all things. I remember what it is like to be human, but I have assumed the position of what it is like to be God. I want to love and heal my world. Compassion is the motivating force in my life.

Can Christians be Saved?

Virginia's Ritual—Buck Speaks

To me, the Crucifixion is now the death and surrender of the long-held collective belief in the dualistic God of the Old Testament. If we let go of the view that the gospels present an accurate account of historical events, then what should we make of what these powerful stories were designed to teach us? If the God of Love or Oneness does not require sacrifices, then the story of the Crucifixion could be seen as representing symbolically the death of the idea that God is judgmental and demands sacrifices. The God of the tree of the knowledge of good and evil is killed upon the tree (the Cross)! Giving up something that the collective human mind has held onto so tenaciously (however unconsciously) for ages certainly could be painful, even horrifying. We humans tend to become identified with our pains and pathologies. We are often loath to give them up because without them, we simply don't know who we are. So the collective mind would probably hold onto its pains and pathology in the same way. Learning the story of the Crucifixion while still carrying the dualist mindset and while believing that the Bible is history would preclude interpreting the Crucifixion symbolism as is done herein. This is fine; this entire narrative has been about taking responsibility for our own interpretations of things. We invite you to come to your own conclusions. To me, the Cross is the killing tree upon which Jesus suffered while his dualistic thinking was symbolically destroyed. This was the killing of a long-held belief. Can I make a similar transition?

What does the Resurrection symbolize? Shouldn't it be the arising of the New Testament God, the God of Love and Oneness? And in my personal vision of Jesus in the Garden of Eden, I sit at His right hand. It is my personal experience that makes these ideas believable for me.

In this interpretation, the story of the death and resurrection of Jesus is the story of our individual conversion from duality to oneness. We have to bear the Cross until our old beliefs based in duality have been sacrificed.

The gospels present to us a Jesus split between the God of the Old Testament and the new God of Love. In the gospels, Jesus often speaks first as one and then as the other—until after the Resurrection. Now there is only one god, the God of Love. The first teaching following the Resurrection that Jesus makes to His disciples is to be forgiving.

> *"If, within yourself, you are able to unlock your heart's doors and send away your feelings of judgment over differences with others and over being wronged, then your heart will be free. If, however, you do not choose to release yourself, then the trespasses you hold against others will remain alive, held fast within you and in the world."*[66]   JN 20²³ 'y u forgive sins' any ...
> ... retain ..

— *Alexander J. Shaia & Michelle Gaugy*

Like the Jesus of the New Testament, and even with these new experiences, I still catch myself speaking with two voices. But I now have set the intention to stop thinking and speaking judgmentally so characteristic of the archetype of the judgmental and patriarchal God of the Old Testament.

The symbolism of the transition in human consciousness from duality to oneness in North America took place about 900 years before the first European settlers arrived in the so-called New World in the story of Hiawatha. Hiawatha selected the biggest tree in the forest. Working together with others, he was able to dig it up by hand and topple it. Then he and his companions threw all their instruments of war into the hole and buried them. Then a new tree was planted where the old tree had stood. This tree grew into the Great Tree of Peace, which we could see as the tree of life. Hiawatha's culture shifted from one of inter-tribal wars to that of the peaceful Iroquois Confederacy.

---

66 Alexander J. Shaia & Michelle Gaugy: *The Hidden Power of the Gospels* (New York, NY: HarperOne, 2010), p. 225. This passage is based on a translation of John 20:23, as expanded and interpreted.

The God Position—Buck Speaks

A significant discovery that resulted from the death-resurrection ritual that Virginia and we, her close friends, experienced was a change in Virginia. She identified this as taking on the God position. Her ego receded far into the background of her consciousness. The glow of divinity and a universality of her viewpoint become obvious.

What is the state of consciousness that Virginia refers to as the God position? Beginning students of the Oneness University are often asked to feel the presence of the Divine within. Many of us did begin to have an inkling of this. With practice, this became easier. Eventually, experiencing the presence of the Divine within was virtually constant. Nonetheless, ego often remains in the foreground: First I'm Buck; and then I'm Buck, but aware of the presence of the Divine. Another step waits, according to Bhagavan, when I'll no longer be Buck. I'll become the *anteryamin*, indweller in the heart, which is also called the witness. In this state of awareness, I'll be watching what that character, Buck, is doing. I wonder whether this is the same as the God position. As of today, I still hold onto plain old Buck as my primary identity, even though I'm having increasingly frequent glimpses of a higher state of being such as at the end of the Last Supper Ritual, Part 2.

I suspect that each of us may have our own unique pathway up the ladder of consciousness. I do hold the intention of seeking evolution of my consciousness. I do this by several methods: setting this as an intention; personally experiencing the scriptures as allegories or initiations; giving and receiving the oneness blessing; and paying attention to what I'm thinking, saying, and doing. I am especially watchful, trying to catch myself shifting into duality. When I catch myself making judgments, this is a reliable indicator that I'm in duality, with ego in charge.

Discussion of Initiations

In the second or third century BCE, the Hebrews, dreaming and longing for a messiah, may have done a crucifixion and resurrection ritual to acknowledge the need for a savior or messiah. Eventually, this was assigned to the historical Jesus when some believed that a messiah had come and that the world had already been saved. In this great knowledge, they then could believe in the new world and in everlasting life, as many would who came to believe in the name of Jesus. However, because they did this, they missed the point of the ritual, instead establishing a God to worship out there, when the point of the ritual was to divine the holy place inside each of us.

Virginia Speaks

In ancient times, initiation rituals were often performed in the mystery schools. They were vehicles to higher states of consciousness. Modern initiations include degrees conferred by educational institutions. The degree represents the recognition of the achievement of a level of proficiency in a field of study. In the ancient mystery schools, initiations also represented proficiency. However, in addition to gaining knowledge, the initiate was expected to evolve and change his or her consciousness, to attain a degree of enlightenment, or to find fire, as Prometheus did, and return to bring it to the people who were suffering from the cold. As a graduate of a mystery school, the student found that all fear was gone, that elemental forces of the earth could be guided by his/her intention, and that maintaining a heart of love and compassion could purify personal motives. The graduate was a healer, a minister, and a teacher, but also much more than that. Their intention was to shape the world for the better.

The Egyptians performed initiations on their candidates for the priesthood. These initiations often assisted the student in conquering fear. The Egyptians believed that travel to the higher dimensions was possible and that feelings were made manifest like intentions, so that if one was journeying in another world and felt fear or gave into fear that the fear would become part of the world of the initiate and lead to failure.

The initiations consisted of giving the student a seemingly dangerous task. To complete the task, the student would have to conquer his or her fear. One of the initiations was held at the Temple of Kom Ombo, where the student had to swim into a very narrow well and was told that he or she could not exit through the entrance. So the initiate had to swim down until reaching the bottom and finding a passage to the next room. But as the initiate entered and looked up for the light, he or she saw two crocodiles swimming in the water. The initiate had to face this fear to swim up and pass beside the crocodiles to exit the pool, only to be told, "You have failed the initiation! You have chosen the wrong way out." So the students had a year to think it over and decide on another course of action before they tried the initiation pool again. Yes, there was another passage found farther on the bottom of the pool, which took them to safe ground away from the crocodiles. To pass this test, the initiates had to face their fear of the unknown, face their fear of drowning, face their fear of being eaten by crocodiles, and face their fear of failure (for the year between the tests).

Another initiation was at the well at the bottom of the Great Pyramid. The students had to crawl through a very narrow passage and sit in a small space in darkness for several days. The space of the passage was irregular, and it is said that they experienced vertigo and dizziness, all while in the blackest of darkness, surrounded by unyielding stones.[67]

There was another initiation ritual, in which initiates had to lie down in the sarcophagus in the King's Chamber, where it is said that there were beams of light-energy that passed through the initiate's head. Using their training, they then spiraled their consciousness out of their body to journey through the universe and experience actually becoming the Universe. At the end of two days, the initiate had a choice: remain in the universe or return to earth. Part of the training was to want to return to contribute to evolving human consciousness. In Mahayana Buddhism, the one who has attained this state is known as a bodhisattva.

So we see that the initiations of the ancient mystery schools contained lessons and tests that presented timeless truths. The shaman's

---

67 Selections explaining temple initiation are from Drunvalo Melchizedek: *Ancient Secret of the Flower of Life* (Flagstaff, AZ: Light Technology Publishing, 2000), Vol. II, pp. 262–268.

intention is to bring truth to the world, yet to walk into the place where the fire is requires that one knows oneself. The ancient initiations taught above all to remove all hidden things inside oneself, to confront each of them, and to be transformed.

All of us have experienced spiritual transitions. Such an initiation may have happened as a result of an unusual event: when a loved one died, when we fell in love, or when we experienced an overwhelming oneness with nature. It could have been when we felt a new direction in our lives and celebrated the event with ritual. In any case, the result of the initiation was a change in our spiritual consciousness and a wonderful feeling that all things are possible.

Jesus experienced an initiation when he was tempted in the wilderness. Before that experience, he was baptized. His baptism celebrated the passage from his preparation to his public ministry.

The initiation in my life that I will never forget was when I crossed genders. During my transition to living as a woman, I had to face my fears: the fear of losing my job, the fear of losing family and friends, the fear of losing my reputation, and possibly even the fear of losing my life. In Buddhism, these fears arise because we have attachments to things in our lives because of our desires. As I faced those fears and walked through each of them to the other side, I entered a new spiritual world. Once in that new world, I could marvel at the moonset and the sunrise, and I could feel spiritual alchemy come alive to change the world. I knew that all things are possible.

In the Old Testament, when persons would have a spiritual experience with God, they would build an altar out of stone. That altar would exist for all of their life to remind them of the experience, lest they forget. Allegorically, this means that when we have those spiritual experiences (initiations) that change our lives that we should never forget. Even on the days when we feel far from godlike, we can remember the divine experience and consider the experience more real than our feelings. In this way, our change is permanent. There is no going back. Experiencing initiations is a wonderful blessing and affirmation that we are evolving spiritually into oneness.

✲✲

Chapter 6

Spiritual Tools to Oneness

When he (Jesus) was alone, the others around him asked him about the parables. He told them, "The secret of the kingdom of God has been given to you. But to those on the outside, everything is said in parables so that they may be ever seeing, but never perceiving, and ever hearing, but never understanding; otherwise, they might turn and be forgiven!"[68]

I am a church official; realizing that we, the clergy, are facing the significant possibility that the gospels are going to be made public soon. After considering this problem for some time, it occurs to me to make Jesus responsible for keeping sacred truths secret for so long within church archives. I can do this by simply adding a few verses in key places within the scriptures, attributing them to Jesus Himself. I am so proud

---

68 Mark 4:10.

of having this clever idea. One of these insertions I place in the Gospel of Mark (quoted above) and several in the Gospel of Matthew; in one, I refer back to the respected prophet Isaiah[69] to make it sound really authentic.

—Buck as a Catholic official in times past

So we, Virginia and Buck, as we compose the words of an imaginary plotting church official, somewhere back in time, are critical, judgmental, sneaky, and ambitious, just as this imagined church official was. Certainly we are not practicing the spiritual tools to oneness until we each realize: "I Am That."

We offer these spiritual tools to you, the reader, to help you realize the state of oneness. However, we realize that many of you already have your own tools or ideas on how to do this. The effectiveness of the tools will vary from individual to individual. These examples have worked for us, and we hope that they will be meaningful to you. The four tools are:

1. Nonjudgment
2. Identification with the suffering of the world
3. I Am That!
4. God realization

Tool 1. Nonjudgment

Judgment sustains duality.

—Robert Zaring

---

69 Matthew 13:34–36.

Virginia Speaks

I am eating at a sidewalk café. A family is sitting at a table close to my table. I can overhear all of this family's conversation. The woman is speaking; she is saying how the country is heading into an abyss because of Obama's presidency. Immediately, I start thinking how stupid this woman is and how wrong she is. I wonder how many other foolish ideas she has. Then as I realize what I am doing. I pull myself back from my own abyss and consider that the woman is my sister; she deserves my compassion, respect, and love. In fact, I consider how the two of us are one.

—Virginia observing herself

I remember that the method for freeing myself from viewing the world judgmentally is to give attention to what I feel. When I notice such a judgmental feeling start to arise, this feeling places me against a person—what the person is saying or doing, I can stop what I am doing and examine my thoughts. Then I can choose to change my thoughts from comparison to compassion for the person, as well as compassion for myself. Oh, this truly brings in the light.

When I, like many of us in the West, hear the word *nonjudgment*, often I have been smitten with incredulity, for I was, as was almost everyone else, immersed in a culture in which I was taught to judge everything that I saw and experienced. Automatically, I have labeled things *good* and *bad*, *good* and *evil*, or *right* and *wrong*. I regularly assign things grades (A, B, C, D, or F). I have compared the actions of others against my own. I have judged whether this one or that one is worthy of my association, my friendship, or even my love. I have assigned value judgments to persons I've encountered and events that I've observed. And by no means should I have shunned some of these sensory inputs, for I have felt a need to make decisions based upon relevant criteria. But there is a reason why all major spiritual disciplines, religions, and philosophies issue warnings if not prohibitions against judging one's fellow beings. From "Judge not lest ye be judged" in the Bible,[70] to the Buddhist imperative of nonjudgment leading to a heart of compassion, I have seen that the principle of nonjudgment is one that religion has characterized as a virtue.

The Buddhist monk Mu Soeng said, "There are many tools of transformation, but the only place where transformation really takes place is in the human heart." Judgment of others takes us out of heart space. We enter the place of believing that we are better than that which we judge. If not that, then we enter a place in which we consider the negativity of the act and are drawn away from our place of peace and into a place of despair or disturbance.

In experience-based spirituality, when I have an archetype of Jesus, Buddha, or Gandhi living in my heart, then I act, think, and believe out of that **nature**. My nature is to bless and heal, not to judge others. By blessing and healing, I am not centering my life (my thinking) on a set of rules (do this, but don't do that); instead, my actions are a result of who I am in my spiritual core, or the experience that I have had with an archetype, a philosophy, or a teaching. If I am a Christian, but have not experienced Jesus, then I simply adhere to a set of rules in a two-thousand-year-old book.

We have to stop comparing ourselves with others. Each soul is on its own individual journey in the collective consciousness. Comparisons hurt the soul and heart. Comparison makes you think that you are better or worse than someone else. Our God-self doesn't see it this way. We must keep our focus on ourselves and our own transformation, not on others and what others are doing.

I used to believe that those who did not believe the way I did would be punished horribly in hell for eternity. Indeed, the Christian verbiage that some are _saved_, while others are _unsaved_, refers to being saved from eternal damnation. This belief leads to dividing the world into "us" and "them," right and wrong, saved and damned. This presupposes that if I am on the saved side, then I am better

---

70 Matthew 7:1.

than those on the other side; after all, I am on God's side, while they are on Satan's side. This is probably the most extreme and visible example of living one's life by judgment. This is not the way Jesus and God (all divine consciousness) meant for us to view the Creation and the beings that inhabit it.

What happens in our minds and hearts when we judge others or events in our lives? Judgment is the opposite of acceptance. Acceptance is a peaceful action, friendly to my heart. Judgment is a violent action and predisposes assuming that others or their actions are wrong.

By accepting what shows up in my life, I am merely acknowledging what is. This person or that event shows up in my life. That's what is. Nothing is "right or wrong" or "good or bad" in and of itself. It's just what is at that point in my life. Greg Braden says, "We witness all events, those of environmental balance and those that we see as the absence of this balance, as possibilities—without judgment of right, wrong, bad, or good."[71]

Can you begin to see how, by using the tool of acceptance, that you can start to eliminate the value judgments of right and wrong from the people and events that show up in your life? Greg Braden says again, "We release our judgment of the situation by blessing those conditions that have caused us pain. The blessing does not condone or consent to the event or condition. Rather, it acknowledges that the event is part of the single source of all that is."

Judging is a concept rooted in the fear-based paradigm of separation. Acceptance originates in the love-based paradigm of oneness. In oneness, we accept and bless all the people and events that show up in our lives as different aspects of our individual and joint creations. On an esoteric level and on a practical level, this is doable[72].

If we feel regret, sorrow, anger, or resentment toward current or past events, circumstances, or people in our lives, then we are in a state of judgment. When we are in this state, our thoughts and feelings are based on negativity or lack. Our mind asks, "What did

---

71 Greg Braden. http://www/spiritofmaat.com/aug1/gb_modes.html

72 Richard Blackstone: Acceptance is the Spiritual Key to Non-Judgment, http://1stholistic.com/reading/prose/A2007/acceptance-is-the-spiritual-key.hlm

I do wrong?" "What did I miss?" "What did I not do, or not do enough of?" or "Am I good enough?" Our mind and emotions can also try to blame others or circumstances for what went wrong or for what's missing. If we apply a judgment system of good and bad to ourselves, then we project that out to others and the world, seeing them as good or bad. Can we see that this creates a cycle of guilt, regret, sorrow, and anger that we associate with our lives, which we then project onto our family, coworkers, and friends? We are living dysfunctional lives because of our judgments of people and events in our lives.

Buddhists, in understanding impermanence, strive for nonjudgment. When one is immediately focused in present experience, what is central is the experience itself, not some judgment or thought about it. Usually, indulging in judgment about an experience is a clue that one is not finding composure in [one's heart] impermanence, but has strayed from being in the moment into past or future, hope or fear. In fact, judgmentalism usually interferes with the vividness of the experience itself, distancing one from its immediacy and raw power. This is why value judgments and determinations that something is good or bad are relatively unimportant to Buddhists.[73]

Buck and I have practiced realizing when we judge and sitting with our feelings about this, accepting ourselves, and then moving into acceptance. Acceptance does not mean that we necessarily approve of or condone the action that we have witnessed; acceptance means that we acknowledge that this event is in our lives. Should we take an action in the moment? Should we move to bless someone? Should we move to heal a person or move to encourage, love, or have compassion? When we have value judgments about a woman yelling and slapping her child in the supermarket, we are frozen with our judgment and are unable to move with compassion. Perhaps compassion would tell me to pray for the woman, or perhaps compassion would tell me to buy a flower and give it to her. Perhaps compassion

73 Rita M. Gross: *Impermanence, Nowness and Nonjudgment: A Personal Approach to Understanding Finitude in the Buddhist Perspective*, Ch. 12 in *Roger Reed Jackson*, Impermanence, Nowness and Non-judgment: Personal Approach to Understanding Finitude in Buddhist Perspective. p.252

would offer me a way to bless her. In this way, we become givers of life and blessings—not judgers. Hooray!

One of Don Miguel Ruiz's students says it this way: "The intent of nonjudgment is to have enough awareness that you know when you are starting to judge someone else or yourself. You know when you are being too hard on yourself. You know when your expectations of yourself are too high, and you are setting yourself up for self-judgment when your expectations are not fulfilled. As you become aware of judgment, the intent is to shift yourself into nonjudgment."[74]

We are frequently our own harshest judges. We may have a standard for perfection for ourselves that approaches some of our archetypes. As we practice nonjudgment of ourselves, we truly can be transformed in our heart to love ourselves. Once this happens, then loving and accepting others becomes possible.

During those years when I was a Christian pastor, I preached a harshly judgmental message against persons who were unsaved and against groups of people that my doctrine considered damned according to the scripture. These groups included gays, Buddhists, Democrats, and all the other groups that did not adhere to fundamentalist teaching. I had chosen to believe dogma over experience in my life. Despite adhering for years to that way of being in the world, I walked out of that way of thinking and into a world of nonjudgment and oneness. In dealing with the cultural shame of being transgender, I saw that I needed to be understanding, forgiving, and accepting of others. In walking through the shame that I was different from most other people, I learned to love myself as I was. I realized one day that if I could love myself and rise above the cultural shame, then I could also forgive and love others. In this way, I was led away from the dogma path and into a path toward the oneness of all things.

We can be present with those with whom we have differing opinions, without clouding our thoughts with judgment of them. How else can we act and move in love and compassion?

---

74 Dona Bernadette Vigil: *Mastery of Awareness,* Bear and Co. Rochester, Vermont, p.99

By watching and considering our thoughts, we can measure whether our hearts and minds are in duality and judgment or in oneness and compassion. Toltec wisdom calls this "stalking" our thoughts. We have seen that watching our thoughts of judgment and nonjudgment can be transformative in leading us to a mind of love and compassion.

Buck Speaks

So after a lifetime of making decisions based on the automatic judgments that I've been making all my life, what do I do when I awaken to an observation that I've already started to judge someone or something? How do I arrive at a decision as to what action to take in the face of this particular experience? Stepping back mentally, I often realize that I have no need to make a judgment about what is before me, and I further realize that if I do make a judgment, then I'm likely to keep on wondering whether I've made the right judgment. Finally, I realize that all of this mental activity accomplishes nothing, but it does use up a bunch of time and energy that I could better enjoy if invested elsewhere.

What if I believe that I really need to make a judgment? Right now, I'm having no luck in recalling such a situation in recent times. What I do recall is celebrating not having to waste energy making a useless decision.

But I don't think I'm wishy-washy either. I can easily say that I want to do this or that I don't want to do that. This doesn't seem to be a judgment; it simply feels as if I'm expressing my feelings.

I have made a concerted effort to give up making judgments. But I do not belittle myself when I catch myself automatically responding according to my old programming. After all, haven't I found many judgmental statements attributed to Jesus before his resurrection? For example, even at the Last Supper, Jesus is said to have quoted an Old Testament judgment when speaking of his impending betrayal.[75]

---

75 "The Son of Man indeed goes just as it is written of Him, but woe to that man by whom the Son of Man is betrayed! It would have been better for that man if he had never been born" (Matthew 14:21).

In giving up judgments, I am giving up duality. Sometimes, I feel lost because I am so habituated to using judgments to make decisions, but if I am love, can't I simply trust my intuition and no longer have to use my old belief filters?

Buck Continues: Noticing Balance Instead of Making Self-Judgment

A practice of oneness that is a useful alternative to self-judgment is noticing whether or how we are out of balance. For each of the chakras, the extremes of being out of balance have been defined. It is helpful to give attention to each of these seven aspects of our personal functioning. These aspects are given in the following table. This is taken from the teachings of the Oneness University.[76]

Chakra	One Extreme	Other Extreme
1. Perineum	Certainty	Uncertainty
2. Sexual area	Indulgence	Abstinence
3. Abdomen	Dominance	Subservience
4. Heart	Possessiveness	Indifference
5. Throat	Resignation	Extreme seeking
6. Third eye	Carelessness	Perfection
7. Crown	Analysis	Synthesis

As I watch myself, I notice that in some these seven areas, I tend to position myself in one or the other of these extremes. And in the crown chakra, I'm often doing both analysis and synthesis, which is exactly what I need to do when I am in the position of the Virgo scientist. However, at many other times, being a scientist is really off-balance.

---

76 This practice is the Charka Dhyana including Bhagavan's corresponding teachings, See Appendix 3, page 229.

The twelve apostles define the other polarities in which it is easy to get off-balance. For example, as Philip the Virgo, I am likely to forget the utility of my intuition and find myself relying solely on rational thought.

The key for me is to recognize the many polarities that are available to me and to pay attention from the polarity that I am using, and then checking whether this is OK. That gives me more options. Consciously choosing to move a balance point, with practice, seems much easier than making judgments. This is a big part of my spiritual practice.

Tool 2. Identification with the Suffering of the World

"Anything experienced fully becomes joy"

—*Sri Bhagavan*

Virginia Speaks

We hear often of terrible things: Hurricane Katrina, earthquakes, tsunamis, and fires that kill and injure numerous people. Catastrophes will occur, and we have to deal with these events with compassion and help. But it is not these types of suffering that we address in this chapter. The suffering that we discuss herein is what we all experience. Jesus said:

> *Therefore I tell you, do not worry about your life, what you will eat or drink; or about your body, what you will wear. Is not life more important than food and the body more important than clothes? Look at the birds of the air; they do not sow or reap or store away in barns, and yet your heavenly Father feeds them. Are you not much more valuable than they? Who of you by worrying can add a single hour to his life?*[77]

—*Jesus*

---

77 Matthew 6:25–27.

This teaching parallels the Buddha's teaching of the Four Noble Truths. We all suffer when our thoughts control us and lead us to their inevitable conclusions. This thought scenario has occurred in many events and in many times in our lives.

> **My boss looked at me strangely today. I do not think that he likes me. In fact, he is going to fire me. Then I will be out of a job and will not be able to find another because of the economy. My family and I will lose the house, and we will be miserable. Oh, what should I do?**
>
> **—Virginia**

Thought patterns like this one make us miserable. When we act these out many times in a day, it is no wonder that we all need a personal therapist. This is the suffering that we must address. Another example of this is the joy and disaster cycle of living. We go through life seeking joyful experiences and fearing and avoiding disaster. In this way, our happiness is contingent upon our surroundings and having good experiences.

When I was a fundamentalist Christian, I remember suffering terribly with thoughts of: "Am I good enough? Is this thing I am doing a sin? How can I stop doing this sin in my life? Does God forgive me?"

My salvation would come from something outside myself, but thinking that would only quiet such thoughts for a moment. The cycle of sin, death, guilt, and fear was an integral part of my thinking, as well as the preposterous notion that we are all born with a sin-nature. Placing salvation in one person who lived two thousand years ago is convenient, heroic, and consistent with some other God-man myths, but misses the experiential component of allowing the God-nature in me to ascend in my life.

When we become aware of the suffering of the world, then we begin a journey back to the tree of life. We first see our lives transformed to be free of worry and stress, and then we release our intentions to alleviate the suffering of the world. This is Christ-consciousness; this is the heart of the Bodhisattva.

I realized this as the God Position after the ritual I did of death and rebirth. As I contained and felt the suffering of my transgender family, I felt the horrible suffering that most of us (maybe all) go through. As I then gave the suffering over to the altar of Ereshkigal, I lost my attachment to the suffering. After this, I was still acutely aware of the suffering of transgender people, but I realized that I was no longer subject to and at the mercy of events that cause such suffering. I was free of the suffering, so I turned my attention to those who were still suffering.

The God-men and women in myth and in history had this same identification with the suffering of the world. Instead of their being gods and goddesses whom we should worship, they are patterns and examples that we should follow. We can all have the God Position.

An everyman myth is a story that has a moral that applies to every one of us as we identify with the characters. This is the meaning of the God-man stories and myths. It is left for us to internalize their stories as our own and to live their example in the world. I believe that this is a higher form of honor than giving them my worship and praise. If I seek to live as they do, then this is the highest honor that I can give them.

A great spiritual tool is to consider the suffering of the world. You can do it the way I did by identifying with the suffering of a group, perhaps an ethnic group or a nationality. You can do a ritual or ceremony of your intention, or you can make it a daily intention in your spiritual life. Or you can even identify with a person that you know and hold a sacred space for their enlightenment or awakening. As you do this, identifying with other people in the world, you will begin to lose your separateness from them. You will consider and realize that you are they and they are you. This is a wonderful exercise to realize oneness.

This works like most other spiritual practices. You begin to practice it. You learn the practice completely in time until it becomes a part of your life. Then one day, your thought life catches up to your practice, and you realize that you have been changed. In this way, we can have spiritual intentions for others and not have the suffering of worry, guilt, shame, and fear.

> *Where there is perfection and unity, there can be no suffering. The capacity to suffer arises where there is imperfection, disunity, and separation from an embracing totality. . . . For the individual who achieves unity within his own organism and union with the divine Ground, there is an end of suffering. The goal of creation is the return of all sentient beings out of separateness and that infatuating urge-to-separateness, which results in suffering, through intuitive knowledge into the wholeness of eternal Reality.*[78]

—*Aldous Huxley*

Buck Speaks

My father has had a major heart attack and is not expected to recover. I go the hospital and come to him bedside. The takes my hand and says: "Buck, I love you but don't approve of the way you live your life." My feelings are all a jumble. I really didn't want to hear the last words from my father whom I love and greatly respect. My old self-judgment: It's not O.K. to me roars through my body. I also think: "My father has his opinion; I have mine." But this thought doesn't remove my pain.

---

78 Aldous Huxley: *The Perennial Philosophy* (New York, NY: Harper and Row, 1944), p. 227.

Can Christians be Saved?

**—Buck meeting with his father
on his deathbed[79].**

I suffer when I feel that it's not OK to be me. I suffer when I feel shame or guilt. I suffer when I feel sorry for myself. I suffer when I feel overwhelmed by anger or fear. And I suffer when I am depressed. When any suffering arises in me, I use the oneness technique of completely getting into the suffering and simply allowing myself to suffer intensely. An example of this was when I took on a friend's feelings of his inner child not being able to trust him (this was told in the story of Abraham). In less than a day, this suffering was completed, and joy returned.

Standing in for Others Leads to Oneness

eg, reciting Po 6 v Dave + Jan Roberts

The root of compassion is not empathy, that's kindness. That's great, but it is not the ultimate compassion. The ultimate compassion is the act which has the potential to relieve every level of suffering. It relieves the suffering that comes from separateness. The suffering that comes from separateness is relieved only when you are fully present with another person, not when you are separately present.

—Ram Das

Virginia Speaks:

In the summer of 2010 I had the opportunity to facilitate the ritual from the death and resurrection chapter for a group of transgender people. During the experience I discovered that I had entered

---

79 Fortunately he didn't die and later things became better between us.

into a state of non-duality. This inspired me to want to articulate what happens in a non-duality state within ritual space.

> Several weeks after my ritual (in Chapter 5), I walk into a meeting of transgender people and as I sit here listening, I find myself looking at this particular person. Suddenly I realize: "I stood for you." I stood for you in sacred space I recall. I walked the circles of suffering, detachment, and rising into newness...for you. I understand that my experience somehow had affected this person. My overwhelming feeling is that I was ONE with her and I still am! Our separation has ended!
>
> Soon I am to realize that this will happen to me quite often, and my first reaction will be to cry with the joy and gratitude for this experience. "I stood for you" will come into my awareness repeatedly. In time as this goes on, I will began to see all people in view of this daily mantra. This will become my practice of recognizing oneness with all people. As I sit with the feeling of the mantra, it allows me to completely let the ego recede, and the joy and gratitude in oneness to be brought forth.

> —Virginia at a meeting

In standing for other people, whether they are an individual, or a group, or a nationality, we experience non-duality. Because we are focused on the well-being of others, and the healing and transformation of others, we begin to feel a oneness with them. This feeling is enhanced as we intend our unconditional love and Divine's grace for them. We ask that we substitute ourselves for them so they may find healing and transformation. Many times we may find ourselves weeping and crying out for their transformation just as they might be doing for themselves. This experience of non-duality in ceremony becomes a feeling of expansiveness, a feeling that I am larger and bigger than myself. My ego and my personality fade as my love and compassion for them comes to the forefront. To me this experience is God Realization.

Buck Speaks

After contemplating Virginia's realization of the result of standing in for others in ritual space, I began to consider the allegory of Jesus standing in for all humankind in his death and resurrection. We had already come to the understanding that he made the final and complete shift from being a Son of the Old Testament God to becoming the Son of the New Testament God of Love during this event. So, I realized that the very act of standing in for everyone was what allowed him to experience all of humankind's suffering. By experiencing this suffering completely he was able to turn it into joy. And joy is our salvation. He didn't do this **for** us; he did it **as** us. We have been asked to believe in Him for salvation. But, I now believe that the truth is that we have to believe in ourselves. We need to realize our divine selves. And we can do this by following the model set by Jesus. He is the archetype of the savior, the one who is willing and able to experience true Oneness with all of us and willing and able to experience all of humankind's suffering.

Thus for me, a deeper interpretation of the fundamental Christian belief that Jesus died on the cross for the sins of others arises from this experience of standing in for others. In the framework of non-duality, this allegory of the crucifixion is a ceremony of becoming at one with all humankind. This is quite different than the dualistic understanding that the god of duality, Jehovah, requires punishment for our sins. Empathy and love for others replaces judgments and punishments.

Tool 3. I Am That!

Virginia Speaks

At the Oneness University in India, one of the teachings is *"Tat Tvam Asi,"* which means "I Am That." This is a statement of nonduality: that I am one with all things, that I am one with God. It also means that the things that I see and judge are mirrors of my soul. And this mirror is reflective of my inner state of consciousness. The things that I do not like about myself I view harshly in others. The ego loves to blame others rather than to confront its own failings. By saying "I Am That," I am saying that I am the thing that I judge. I am the anger, I am the lie, and I am the bitterness. By saying that, its power over me is broken and it becomes an observation of my life, not a judgment of others or myself. "I Am That" is a powerful statement of spiritual recognition of my responsibility over my own life.

"I Am That" also means that as my friend rejoices, so do I. It means that I am a participant in all that I observe, but I am not attached to what I see. Having no attachment means that I have no expectation or wish for the events in my life to move this way or that way. The events just are what they are.

The principle of "I Am That" is as old as humankind's search for meaning, but there is a well-known twentieth-century text by Nisargadatta Maharaj that expounds on the principle. It is entitled *I Am That.*[80] Sri Nisargadatta found self-realization by considering the question "Who am I?" As he meditated on "I am," he came to realize that he was a watcher or observer of the events in his life through his body's senses, and he said that he was "not moved, either to happiness or sadness, based upon what it sees."

I also am the watcher and observer of my world, but I choose to feel the happiness or sadness of others as if it were my own. In this way, I am a compassionate observer. I think it is important that we establish that enlightenment is not walking around in a cloud or in a dispassionate manner. In fact, it can be said that a self-realized person is the ultimate participator in life and in the movements of

---

80 www.fixdisease.com/i_am_that.pdf

spiritual energy in the world. In years past, seekers would look for teachers or gurus to help them on the path to enlightenment. Others withdrew from the world to follow some form of ascetic practice to lead them to self-realization. In the present day, gurus and the ascetic life are not necessary for those who seek self-realization or enlightenment. The process and tools that we have presented in this book are not new. The enlightened person feels joy and sadness, and the enlightened person knows himself or herself. There are no more games, fears, control, or manipulations. The enlightened person can say, "I Am That!"

> The seeker is he who is in search of himself. Give up all questions except one: "Who am I?" After all, the only fact you are sure of is that you are. The "I am" is certain. The "I am this" is not. Struggle to find out what you are in reality. To know what you are, you must first investigate and know what you are not. Discover all that you are not—body, feelings, thoughts, time, space, this or that—nothing, concrete or abstract, [that] you perceive can be you. The act of perceiving shows that you are not what you perceive. The clearer you understand on the level of mind that you can be described in negative terms only, the quicker will you come to the end of your search and realize that you are the limitless being.[81]

— Sri Nisargadatta Maharaj

Buck Speaks

When I was doing the forty-day Arica training in the mid-1970s, we were assigned an hour-long daily exercise of walking about downtown Santa Fe doing an "I Am That" practice. We labeled this activity the

---

81   Sri Nisargadatta Maharaj.

"I Am Everything" exercise. When I see someone driving by a car I become the driver or if I see a cat walking across the street, I think: "I Am That."

In the modern-day Avatar training, a version of this exercise is used to get us out of our minds and into our feelings. In this process, I may see a bird and imagine that I am that bird. I see a tree and become the tree, feeling myself dancing in the wind and my leaves soaking up the sunlight. I may feel a bird sitting on one of my branches. Or I may notice that someone is enjoying my shade.

Thus the "I Am That" not only helps us to establish a oneness point of view of our existence, but also it helps us to get out of our judging minds and into our feeling bodies. It helps us become empathetic and compassionate. It is difficult to get angry at the crowing rooster waking me up too early when I am that rooster because I am to one who is crowing, and I am the one who is announcing "good morning" to the world.

Tool 4. God Realization

"Do you not know that you are gods?"[82]

—*Jesus*

Buck Speaks—The Presence of the Divine within

By experiencing the gospel allegories personally, each of us has had the experience of feeling the presence of God within. In the Oneness University training, the trainers often say, "Experience the Presence." Just what do they mean by this? The answer has to be provided by our own experiences. We have already relayed our stories and referred to the story of Paul's being confronted by Jesus on the road to Damascus. But how can we explain such experiences without

82 John 10:34; Psalms 82:6.

having such an experience ourselves? But, let me give you one more story. This comes from an anonymous author via an e-mail from a friend.

> *Two Americans answered an invitation from the Russian Department of Education to teach morals and ethics (based on Biblical principles) in the public schools. The Americans were invited to teach at prisons, businesses, the fire and police departments, and a large orphanage. About a hundred boys and girls who had been abandoned, abused, and left in the care of a government-run program were in the orphanage. The Americans related the following story in their own words:*

> *"It is nearing the holiday season and time for our orphans to hear, for the first time, the traditional story of Christmas. We tell them about Mary and Joseph arriving in Bethlehem. Finding no room in the inn, the couple goes to a stable, where the baby Jesus is born and placed in a manger.*

> *"Throughout the story, the children and orphanage staff sit in amazement as they listen. Some sit on the edges of their stools, trying to grasp every word. Completing the story, we give the children three small pieces of cardboard to make a crude manger. Each child is given a small paper square, cut from yellow napkins that I brought with me. No colored paper is available in that city.*

> *"Following instructions, the children tear the paper and carefully lay strips in the manger for straw. Small squares of flannel, cut from a worn-out nightgown an American lady was throwing away as she was getting ready to leave Russia, are used for the baby's blanket. A doll-like baby is cut from tan felt that we had brought from the United States.*

> *"The orphans were busy assembling their manger as I walked among them to see whether they need any help. All went well until I got to one table*

where little Misha sat. He looked to be about six years old and had finished his project. As I looked at the little boy's manger, I was startled to see not one, but two babies in the manger. Quickly, I called for the translator to ask the lad why there were two babies in the manger. Crossing his arms in front of him and looking at this completed manger scene, the child began to repeat the story quite seriously.

"For such a young boy, who had only heard the Christmas story once, he was relating the happenings accurately—until he came to the part where Mary puts the baby Jesus in the manger. Then Misha starts to ad-lib. He makes up his own ending to the story. He says, 'When Maria lays the baby in the manger, Jesus looks at me and asks me if I have a place to stay. I tell him I have no mamma and I have no papa, so I don't have any place to stay. Then Jesus tells me that I can stay with him. But I tell him I can't because I didn't have a gift to give him the way everybody else does. But I want to stay with Jesus so much, so I think about what I have that maybe I can use for a gift. I think that maybe if I keep him warm, this will be a good gift.

" 'So I ask Jesus, "If I keep you warm, will this be a good enough gift?"

" 'And Jesus tells me, "If you keep me warm, that will be the best gift anybody ever gave me." So I get into the manger, and then Jesus looks at me and he tells me I can stay with him for always.'

"As little Misha finishes his story, his eyes brim full of tears that splash down his little cheeks. Putting his hand over his face, his head dropped to the table and his shoulders shake as he sobs and sobs.

"The little orphan has found someone who would never abandon nor abuse him, someone who would stay with him—for always."

—author unknown

Can Christians be Saved?

So what do little Misha, Saint Paul, and thousands of others like us have in common? It is a strong connection of our higher consciousness with the Divine. This in turn promotes our seeking of the deep silence of meditation where the great truths of the universe can be brought into awareness. I imagine the aumakua as being light in the night sky—infinitely vast and full of points of consciousness, as the sky has points of light, the stars. I propose that the brightest of these foci of consciousness correspond to spiritual beings, teachers in the spiritual realm.

Jesus Comes to Virginia

One of the advanced Oneness techniques is the dark room meditation, where we fully open ourselves to the presence of the Divine.

I'm sitting in a dark room with a few others in deep silence. Jesus shows up, wearing baggy pants and riding on a skateboard. I realize that I have not seen him since Buck and I were meditating together a few years ago. He says to me, "I am glad that you and Buck have written the book because I'm so friggin' tired of being worshipped as the ONE. It will be nice one day to be included with everyone else. Then I will really feel like the ONE. But I do have one favor to ask: Can you include me in the book?"

I say to him, "But Jesus, you are all through it."

And he says, "No, I mean as you see me now."

And I say, "Hey, it would have been easier if you had told me this several months ago."

And Jesus says, "Just do the best you can."

—Virginia

184

The following morning, I wonder, "Why does he want to be included in the book? I know that he does not have an ego." The only answer I can think of is to make a statement that we are all God, especially those we do not understand or those we think that we don't like as much as we like others. We need to consider everyone we meet as God!

Buck continues

These foci of individual consciousnesses are available to us through our *aumakua*. They can have well-known identities (such as Jesus or Buddha), or they may be unknown to you. Our consciousness can focus on these spiritual beings, and we can communicate with them as we would communicate with good friends. In shamanism, these entities are sought out in the drumming trance journey and identified as our teachers in the higher realm. In shamanism, these beings are tested by asking the following questions:

1. Are you my teacher, guide, or friend?
2. Do you love me unconditionally?
3. Will you always tell me the truth?
4. Will you be available to me when I need you?
5. How do I get in touch with you when I need you?

The answers to these questions must always be an emphatic *yes* for the teacher to be acceptable. Often, the newly discovered teacher is heard to say, either silently or even out loud: "I've been waiting for you to find me all your life."

Some of us, like Misha, Paul and me, have an inner star that we have identified as Jesus. So it just doesn't matter whether Jesus was a real character in history; he exists in the spiritual realm (or the collective aumakua). And he can manifest in our personal experiences, including in the experiences of people who didn't believe in him before such an experience. A further discovery is that these spiritual teachers can be invoked at will with a little practice. To invoke the presence means to us that we are experiencing a conscious awareness of the presence of the Divine within, in the character of a spiritual teacher whom we know and recognize personally. Furthermore, we are not limited to just one such spiritual guide. We may experience a number of such presences. The aumakua is included in the wholeness of God.

Such a spiritual guide or presence does not require worship, as Jesus abruptly announced to Virginia. Rather, what is required is an intimate and loving relationship with the Divine as it arises within us. The Divine is a friend and is not external to us.

Instead of worshiping God, we are now able to enjoy God as we would enjoy a really special friend. And as God is internal, we are never really separated from God. As this god is everything—all life, all energy, all matter—his or her face can be of our own choosing and can change, depending on the situation. Worship has changed to meditation in the presence of this inner divine friend and/or recognizing God in anyone or anything we meet.

Bhagavan of the Oneness University explains it this way:

> The Divine is in you as the Higher Self. You must first become aware of this connection. And then, as you become more and more aware, you must learn to talk to the Divine just as you talk to your father, mother, your friend, your son, or your daughter, not to something called the Divine, but not really personally experienced. This just doesn't work. The Divine must be recognized and personal. It is the kind of individual to whom you can relate without reservation. Just think of the Divine as your father or your friend. Sometimes in India, people even address the Divine as their own servant. It is amazing. The question is: Is there a bond? There must be a bond between you and the Divine. And it must fit into known human frameworks. To simply use the term "God" is not really helpful because God you're not seeing. How do you relate to God? You don't put him into a human mold; it's difficult. So you have to choose whatever relationship is best in your life. For example, if your relationship with your mother is

the best, then cast the Divine as your mother. If it's great with your father, (then cast the Divine) as your father. If it's wonderful with your brother, (then cast It) as your brother or as a friend. But whatever you do, there must be friendship between you and the Divine. And not only that, but also you must cast the Divine in a mold who's not terribly demanding, who's not putting fear into you, (and) who's not awesome. If you portray your Divine as somebody really awesome, you can be sure that you will not be able to relate. You have to envision the Divine to somebody who's personal, who's friendly, (and) who will listen to you.

—Bhagavan, freely translated

And what if you don't believe in God? Belief is unnecessary. Annette Carlstrom[83] explains that atheists like herself often refer to this inner divine presence as the atriamin or inner observer. What is needed is faith in your experiences. Of course it is easy to trick ourselves into believing almost anything—and thereby deceiving ourselves. Deep meditation and contemplation help get at the truth of what experiences can tell us. The best way is to achieve *sunia*, a Sikh term that means silence. Truth arises in silence. Nanak, the first guru of the Sikh religion, taught that the name of God was Truth. Anybody can believe in silence, but it not easy to achieve the state of mental silence. A good meditation teacher can help!

Virginia Speaks

The Indian sages talk of a lump of salt that goes to plumb the depths of the ocean. What happens to it? The lump dissolves in sea-water in no time and becomes one with the ocean. Similarly, knowing God intellectually is impossible; it is only possible by dissolving your identity as the small self into God, becoming God. *Brahma vidam brahamaiva bhavati* (the knower of Brahman becomes Brahman), the Vedas declare.

---

83 http:www.onenessuniversity.org/experiences_video.html

Can Christians be Saved?

The true value of a human being is determined primarily by the measure and the sense in which he has attained liberation from the self.[84]

—*Albert Einstein*

I am on visualization journey, and being challenged to meet my personal goddess.[85] I am led to a wonderful magical and peaceful world. I walk into a sacred space to meet my personal goddess. I am excited to meet my goddess and to spend some time with her in meditation. I step into a golden room with purple drapes and a wonderful picture window looking out onto the garden. Goddess approaches me from behind.

I turn around, and I am staring at me! I am there, and I am here. My Goddess and I are one! I stand weeping at the realization when I, Goddess, walks up to me and puts her arms around me, my arms go around her, and we hug together as if this was the only moment that we would share in our entire existence. All of a sudden, I realize that I know a wonderful secret together with Goddess, and that is that I am She! We both realize it together and start to laugh. We laugh with joy.

—Virginia

My awakening, my liberation from the ego, and my God realization were all life-changing for me. My awakening came about as a direct result of my transition from William to Virginia. By walking through the many fears around my gender transition, I discovered that I saw the world in a different way.

84   Alice Calaprice (Ed.): *The Expanded Quotable Einstein*, Princeton University Press, Princeton, NJ 2000.

85   This happened during a guided medication led by a Oneness trainer, Janice, during a Oneness Awakening Course, in Albuquerque, NM, on July 24, 2010.

My liberation from the ego, specifically the rendering of my ego as irrelevant, is recounted above, in chapter 3, through my experience of becoming at one with Ereshkigal. This was also a sudden realization of oneness. I had felt the union with the universe before, but the experience deepened and became an ever-present reality.

The realization that one is God makes the individual person become unimportant. The ego is entirely uninvolved in God realization. Many people in the West get furious or confused when God realization is mentioned. They say, "How could you think such a thing?" or they assume that the realization of God consciousness means that we feel superior to them, as we say that we are "God" and they say that they could not be God. The irony is that after attaining God consciousness, the last thought I would have is that I am better than anyone else. That thought is rooted in the ego. Did not Jesus say, "Whoever wants to become great among you must be your servant"?[86]

Experiencing God Realization. Becoming God realized is as easy as stepping across a shallow creek and as hard as jumping off a pinnacle. It is accomplished as an act of the will, a spiritual intention to move into the God Position. What am I getting into by choosing God realization?[87]

Something profound seems to be occurring within me. My personality seems to be dismantling before my eyes. I am experiencing my ego as an extremely valuable vehicle with which to negotiate my everyday world, but there is no longer an identification with it. "Janice" is there, but only like a garment that I wear to function in the world of shape and form. Words seem just naturally to arise when I need to talk. The body takes care of itself. If I need to bathe, the body seems to know naturally what to do. If I need to

86 Matthew 20:26.
87 Adyashanti, The End of Your World, Sounds True, Boulder, Co.2010

189

eat, I seem to know what my body wants and go do it, yet sometimes the silence and vastness are so immense that I hear myself say, "Screw it, I'm not eating right now!" Ha! Ha!

I really don't want to go back to identifying with my personality. This feels immense, and I like it. My personality seems to like having the important job of negotiating the material world, but it's not driving the car anymore. I witness myself saying and doing things, and I find this amusing. My mind is disidentified with my thoughts.[88]

—Janice

What things will change? My life will never be the same because I take up the responsibilities of my life. It is the ultimate in personal responsibility. I am now the creator of the events in my life through my intention. I am the watcher and observer of other events and people in my world. I am also the observer of my thoughts, actions, decisions, hopes, and dreams. There is also no one to blame for problems, events, or the situations that arise in my world. There is no one outside myself to ask for a bailout.

With a heart filled with love, compassion, and gratitude, I now believe that the mission of my life is for all people and my world. For the awakening of the world, for each person to be able to receive the Divine's grace.

> We need the willingness to lose our world. That willingness is the surrender; that willingness is the letting go. Each of us has to find what that letting go means for us, what we need to let go of. Whether it's easy or difficult doesn't matter in the slightest. It is the letting go that is ultimately important.
>
> —Adyashanti

---

88 Janice, reporting to friends after a weekend Oneness workshop where she experienced a profound shift in consciousness.

What is your obstacle to God realization? The pinnacle from which I had to jump was my own feeling of unworthiness to be God. All my life, I had been immersed in the principle that there was only one God, out there, and to say I was God would be an affront and an outrage that others would criticize. On the day of my death-and-resurrection ritual, I knew that was what I was afraid of. I was not afraid to die; I was afraid to be resurrected and take the God Position to myself. In ritual space, I was able to confront this within myself, and the Divine took away my unworthiness and gently led me to merge with Divine consciousness so that there was no longer any separation. I am God. I was healed and saved from caring what others think of me. In stepping out to God realization, each person may have a different obstacle with which to deal.

There is doing but no doer. Knowing this, my world has changed. Every person I meet is God. Whether they are at the same place in their path as I am is irrelevant. Comparisons are not real when one is in the God Position. Judgments are not real. When someone comes up to me and compliments me on my spiritual performance in some event, I express thanks and say that I feel loved and supported by that praise. I do not say, "It is just the Divine working through me." I cannot say that anymore because that is not an absolutely true statement. I am in the God Position, and I am witnessing my actions, but there is no doer. My ego is totally uninvolved in my life and in my actions.

Existence, consciousness, and bliss. The knowledge of this, the experience of watching me as God realized, can only be felt as bliss. It is a spring of joy as I am able to experience life fully. But as I watch myself, I realize that I am not watching just myself, but all Creation. There is seeing, but no seer. One of the things that I immediately felt after the ritual was that for the first time, I was a true participant in life. The feeling of being alive is so ever-present the closest word to describe it is *bliss*. Through the activation of my consciousness with the knowledge of existence, one experiences bliss. Existence may be defined as all things, and consciousness would add the component of sentient. The knowledge and experience that I am not separate from the ultimate reality makes me laugh and cry with joy. I am not here. ALL is here.

God realization is the ultimate world-changer. When we realize that we are God, then we accept our responsibility to create solutions to problems and to heal our world and our people from the effects of duality. It is here that we can love and have the power of compassion.

Two trees grew in the garden. The one to which we are returning is the tree of life. This means that the new earth that we will see when the planet is awakened will not be as it is now. If this world were awakened, we would have the power to heal Mother Earth completely. With our intention, we could raise the vibrations and energy to heal and save our waters and our atmosphere. There would be no more wars. We could build parks and schools where the Pentagon used to be. There would be joy in helping the neighbors on our block with their difficulties, and we would not fear to invite a poor person home with us for a meal and a hot bath. Our differences in beliefs would not separate us because we would consider each other like ourselves. This dream of the planet we can realize through oneness.

Empathy and Oneness

I'm listening to the news. What is being reported is that an military psychiatrist has gone on a shooting rampage and has killed many people. I feel anger rising up in me. Then I notice that I'm judging this man, this mass murderer. But I catch myself and by will instruct myself to feel into this person. As I become him, I notice how numb he/I am, how intense the denial is. I then feel under this numbness and denial. What's here deep down? Pain, pain so deep that it is impossible to allow myself to feel it or to know it. My only available response is just to lash out at anyone who is around. I kill without feeling it.

Then I come back into myself. I cry out with this man's unfelt hurt. Now I can't judge me anymore. But I can still cry out for his pain when I recall this event.

—Buck on hearing a newscast

Empathetic moments are the most intensively alive experiences that we ever have. We feel super-alive because in the empathetic act, which begins with being embodied, we transcend our physical confines and, for a brief period, live in a shared noncorporeal plane that is timeless and that connects us to the life that surrounds us. We are filled with life, our own and others', feeling connected and embedded in the here-and-now reality that our relationships create.[89]

—*Jeremy Rifkin*

---

89 Jeremy Rifkin: *The Empathic Civilization: The Race to Global Consciousness in a World in Crisis* (New York, NY: Penguin Group, 2009), p. 164.

Oneness is more than empathy with others; it is empathy with all, including all parts of ourselves, all of Creation, and the Creator. Oneness is a *brief period*, but can transcend boundaries as our consciousness evolves into Christ consciousness. Rifkin expands his explanation of empathy to panentheism by quoting Borg in the book *The God We Never Know.*[90]

> *Panentheism as a way of thinking about God affirms both the transcendence of God and the immanence of God. For panentheism, God is not a being out there. The Greek roots of the word point to its meaning: pan means everything, en means in, and theos means God. God is more than everything (and thus transcendent), yet everything is in God (hence God is immanent). For panentheism, God is right here, even as God is also more than right here.*
>
> —*M. J. Brog*

Oneness is less concerned with defining God and more concerned with how we relate to the Divine. The primary relationships in oneness are with self, our family members, and the Divine. These relationships involve great empathy. Thus empathy with God and experiencing God's empathy with self are what is most important—this is having the experience of empathy with the divine aspect of self. In oneness, it not necessary to believe in God; it is important to experience divinity within the self and as the self. No one in Oneness objects to your being an atheist. Divinity within is comfortably referred to as the *indweller* or the *inner observer*. Sufis call this the *beloved*. Native Americans usually refer to this as Great Spirit.

> *The whole world is family.*
>
> —*Bhagavan*

✽✽

90 Rifkin, *Empathetic Civilization*, p. 171.

Chapter 7

Experience-Based Mystical Christianity

"My religion is simple; my religion is kindness."

—*The Dalai Lama*

Summary of Lessons

We have dissected the writings in the Christian Bible to separate the teachings of the God of Love (New Testament teachings attributed to Jesus when he was speaking as the Son of the God of Love) from the teachings of the God of Judgment (primarily the Old Testament). We have used these sacred texts as teaching allegories or initiations. We have used them to gain personal experiences. When we did this, we found that being a mystical Christian is natural and easy.

This approach was greatly facilitated by the application of the teachings of oneness, which are currently gaining a much wider acceptance among students of spirituality. Below is a list of some of the lessons that we have obtained. We hope that you will determine for yourself whether these lessons reflect your own experiences.

I.   Letting go of beliefs and faith in dogmatic indoctrination: Dogmatic indoctrination negates the validity of our own here-and-now experiences. Beliefs built upon such indoctrination become prisons that limit our awareness of what we are truly experiencing in each moment of our lives. Faith can block us from the truth of our individual experiences.

II.   Experiencing sacred texts as teaching allegories or formulas for personal initiations: We can explore ourselves by unitizing sacred texts as invitations to initiate personal experiences, experiences that can teach us what we are ready to learn. This is different from believing that such texts are the word of God handed down to us by some religion or teacher. When we recognize that God is within us, then we can let our inner God guide us into the true self-understanding of what these sacred texts are able to help us experience. In this way, our own personal experience leads us to beliefs that are true to us rather that beliefs based on someone else's proclamations.

III.   Living in oneness: The story of Creation in the Old Testament of the Bible invites us to examine the two basic worldviews: that everything is one or that everything is separated into good and evil. The great Western religions chose to indoctrinate their followers into the good versus evil view of the world. As most of us grew up within that worldview, we find that we have almost always applied this view. Realizing this, we can invite ourselves to evolve our consciousness to an outlook upon the world of oneness and enjoy the outcome of this way of looking both inside and outside ourselves.

IV.   Utilizing both Christianity and Oneness: When Christianity is studied from the viewpoint of oneness, it becomes easier to see Jesus as the archetype of the Son of the God of Love and as a teacher from the spirit world that has often been present and helpful in the lives of Christians. Jesus is also the archetype of a Christian aspirant who uses personal experiences and initiations to realize that indeed he or is the Son or Daughter of God—the God of Love, not the Old Testament God of Judgment. The identity and presence of Jesus is not limited to an individual residing in a specific time in history. Jesus may be our own face of God within us.

V.   Ending separation; ending duality: As we see ourselves as Christians based on our personal experiences and allow ourselves freedom from beliefs provided to us from dogma and likely inaccurate history and as we find ourselves within the mindset of oneness, we can return to a Christianity with which we can live comfortably; we can have a wonderful relationship with Jesus. However, our image of the God-within is not limited to Jesus, but may be one or more of the great teachers to whom we have been introduced. God's image may even look like us!

VI.   Letting go of worship: When we worship God, we make ourselves inferior to God and take ourselves as being outside God or separate from God. Instead, if we experience God-within as a part of ourselves, then we are one with God. The God-within, or the indweller, becomes an inner beloved who is our most precious friend and has the face of God that is easiest for us to seek. When we are one with God, our relationship with the Divine is a holy friendship, and we experience God as always present, always available, and the one we can trust always to give us unconditional love, always tell us the truth, and never make judgments against us. Worship changes into abiding joy of experiencing the presence of God-within.

VII.   Being nonjudgmental: When we can see the other as self, we can end our contribution to separateness. Judgments are a function of duality; they create separation. In judgment, we not only separate ourselves, but also are likely to feel lonely. We can easily be led to participate in arguments, disagreements, conflicts, and even wars.

Oneness training teaches us that when we become one with the Divine, we can experience immediate and automatic right action. In other words, we simply know what to do and do it. This level of surrender, however, can be scary because we are so accustomed to using our egos to keep us out of trouble, yet as we let our faith grow, based on valid experiences of who we truly are, the possibility of becoming one with the Divine begins to show itself to us. We are able to relax into this way of being in the world. Yes, it is possible to live productively without having to always make judgments to decide what to do.

VIII. Recognizing the difference between nonjudgment and truth telling: It is good for us to appreciate the difference between nonjudgment and truth telling. Judgments are opinions with conclusions. Truth telling is simply reporting back actually what is.

IX. Letting go of having to forgive: To forgive someone assumes that we are putting ourselves somewhat over the other person in a moral sense. This really doesn't end separation. Rather, if we let go of our resentments, our grudges, our jealousies, our anger, or whatever other negativity we are holding onto, something within us changes. We can do this without making ourselves superior to the other. Furthermore, if we put ourselves in the other person's shoes and really understand where the other is or where the other has been coming from, we are doing our part to end separation.

> *The deeper we move into the direct experience of being of the unborn, undying, uncreated that we are, the more we start to move into a true sense of nonduality.*
>
> —*Adyashanti*

X. Experiencing God within: Jesus, speaking as the Son of the God of Love, tells us that we and God are one, that is, that God is within. This gives us a perfect inner companion or friend. However, if our God is the Old Testament God, the God of Judgment,

Punishment, Suffering, etc., then this is the God we want be as far away from as possible; this is certainly not "the God Within" that we would wish to have. Wouldn't this be like living in a prison cell with the warden as our cellmate?

XI.   Standing in non-duality: We can take a role in a ceremony with the intention that we are standing in for others. Thus we do the ceremony not only for ourselves but for others whose intention is like our own. This moves us into non-duality. Because we are also focused on their well-being, and their healing and transformation, we begin to feel a oneness with them. This feeling is enhanced as we extend our unconditional love and Divine's grace to them. Thus we become one with those for whom we are standing. Our consciousness is shifted out of the ego and we find ourselves in the God position.

XII.   Experiencing heaven within: When we fully realize ourselves as having the God of Love within and experiencing ourselves as one with all Creation, we become self-realized or enlightened and live life joyously. This is the heaven to which Jesus (the Son of the God of Love) referred. If you believe in the Old Testament God, then your only way to get to heaven is to die.

XIII.   Forgetting hell: For dualists or fundamentalists, hell, as is heaven, is defined as an after-death state. Unfortunately, living without the God of Love internalized may be experienced as hell on earth. If we are living with an internalized God of Judgment and Punishment as defined in the Old Testament, we probably will find ourselves experiencing hell on earth.

XIV.   Surrendering ego and suffering: Our egos love dualism. Surrendering the ego, which includes a letting go of suffering, allows us to obtain a balance that promotes us into the state of Oneness.

Suffering is not in the fact, but in your perception of the fact.

—Bhagavan

What Is Experience-Based Mystical Christianity?

Virginia Speaks

I am glad to be able to answer this question without dogma. Whenever a new spirituality is suggested often I have seen people start making rules and regulations to control the way the new method is practiced. We will <u>NOT</u> do that. The simple truth is the power of a mystical way is that it is personal for everyone and varies to the individual. Inherent in our process is the experience of internalizing sacred texts, or even day to day events in our lives, to discover who we are, and the essence of our being. My experience will not be yours and yours will not be mine. BUT, we may see intersections and common threads in our experiences which make it exciting to talk about.

Several weeks ago I was asked to attend a group experience where we would all bring a piece of poetry to the meeting. I chose a poem by Rumi, and as I was memorizing it I discovered I was experiencing the poem with the process that Buck and I have practiced. When I arrived at the group and my turn came I told the group I would lead them through my experience with the poem. This is the way it went.

Pay Homage

If God said,
"Rumi, pay homage to everything
that has helped you
enter my arms,"

there would not be one experience of my life,
not one thought, not one feeling, not one act,
I would not bow.

— Rumi

I am now taking the meaning and truth of this poem inside of me, and my intention is that its essence will become part of me, down to the cellular level. I immediately look down a corridor, and I see that it is the hall of my life: the things I have done. I see that some of the events in my life I regret, and some of the events were great successes, but now seeing with the eyes of truth, I see that all of my experiences were the same, they had the same value. They all served to lead me to the Divine within. Realizing this, I am filled with joy and gratitude at the experience.

—Virginia

This to me is how the process of this book has changed me. It lives within me. I have also experienced this process when I have a problem, situation, joy or conflict in my life. The pattern is that first I will fully experience the event and try to FEEL it with the essence of my being. If the event is a disappointment or crisis, I may cry, or be upset, and I give myself permission to do that. I fully experience my distress. Then I place my intention to be open to the divine to teach me, heal me, or instruct me about the situation. I always receive an answer of some sort. Then I have a time of "checking in" with my spiritual guide or teacher about it. Many times that is my higher self, or it may be a close personal friend like Buck is to me, or it may be Ghandi, or Jesus, or maybe AmmaBhagavan. I wait to hear anything they wish to say to me. And then I set my intentions about the matter as a statement of resolve or purpose. After realizing that I have found the answer to the dilemma, I then feel the emotions of joy and gratitude. If the original event is one of joy then I still go through the same steps but I am filled with gratitude in the process.

We have also emphasized and repeated in the book that having a God, or the Divine, who is a close, personal, and loving friend, is invaluable in this process. If you are an atheist or agnostic, perhaps your higher self will be your friend, or the essence of who you are. Whoever your teacher or guide is, there is such great joy in experiencing life with them.

Can Christians be Saved?

What makes our mystical experiences Christian? This is a very subjective experience. If we feel that the Christ consciousness is part of us, or that our personal teacher or guide is Jesus, or that the experience of Biblical stories has brought us to this place, then we can say that this is Christian. If we feel another teacher or religious experience is alive within us we may call it by another name. This is not important. The truth is that the experience lives within us and that we have been transformed in the process. The mystical experience is a universal one, not contained or limited to any one religion or philosophy.

Previously, we have used spiritual words and guideposts to describe our experiences, words like: awakening, enlightenment, and God realization. There is a part of me that wishes we could omit these terms, because they cause many people to be chasing after an experience in the future rather than being present with the joys and journeys of life. They also can serve as words of comparison, as in "she is enlightened and I am not". It is my observation that all these terms can be summed up by the words of a friend, after she experienced a oneness blessing, she said, "**I feel like I am in love with the whole world.**"

When Jesus said "the kingdom of God is within", perhaps some of those listening to him fell in love with the whole world too! The exquisite experience of knowing that God lives through me and in me fills me with joy, and also with love. My love teaches me to accept all people regardless of nationality, ethnicity or gender. My love teaches me to help all those in need, and to stand for those who need God's help. It teaches me to love those who would do me harm, to cherish and nurture my friendships, and to be at One with Divine Consciousness so that there is no separation between us.

These things are what I experience through experience-based mystical Christianity.

Buck Speaks

My original exposure to these Biblical stories caused me to feel uncomfortable because I was taught to believe that they were true but they just didn't sound true to me. Thus I became a sinner by definition simply by studying the Bible. But when I started calling these Biblical stories allegories and started searching into them as being about me not some character in history I started to feel comfortable, inquisitive, and longed to get at their true meaning for me.

My first ah-ha was the investigation of the Christmas story in the Gospel of Matthew. The Gestalt occurred when I relived the story as the baby Jesus. Immediately, I knew that the baby Jesus was my inner child, and I totally fell in love with him. Truly loving and accepting myself occurred right then. I also immediately realized that if I allowed him to grow and remain free of all my adult experiences that would scar my soul; he would become my savior and permit me to experience the world with both his divine innocence and his immersion in God. At this point, I had no doubt that he, just like the allegorical Jesus, was the son of the God of Love. My only sorrow was that I had waited so long in my life before I discovered this awesome fact. Each day now, with giving and receiving more blessings, meetings with Virginia and more Oneness teachings, this experience continues to grow.

I'll end with a prayer: "Thank you, God, for letting me find you inside myself and for being one with me. Thank you for sending Virginia to do this process with me. Thank you for sending the Savior to me, that little baby inner child whom I now know as Jesus, who always walks beside me, is with me, and is me, all grown up—loving me unconditionally, always telling me the truth, and never judging me. And thank you that I don't have to die to live in the joy of heaven. Now I understand what Jesus, the Son of the God of Love in the New Testament, meant when he said: 'The kingdom is within.' For all of this and so much more, I am truly grateful. Amen."

After Moving from Duality to Oneness

When I observe people who routinely receive Deeksha or Oneness blessing, what I notice is that they look and act more joyful. And this joyousness seems to keep on growing. One teacher, when ask about enlightment, responded: "Don't concern yourself with enlightment;

it has too many meanings to really be understood. Instead, ask yourself if you are joyous. Joy is a word you don't have to be concerned about its meaning; you know what it means by how it feels."

> Jesus said to them, "When you make the two one, and when you make the inside like the outside and the outside like the inside, and the above like the below, and when you make the male and female one and the same, . . . then you will enter [the kingdom]"[91]

God is One; God is All

God and I are one,
Successfully initiated into my complete life,
Unmasked and outside all my cages of beliefs,
Free of all attachments, all identities.
One day I fly solo in an airplane at 500 miles per hour
    And have a great time, hands on the controls, fully in charge.
The plane, with all of its controls, simply disappears.
There, discovering that I'm still attached to this body, to this life,
And still believing in gravity,
I realize that to be God, I must let go of these remaining hooks
And simply enjoy the freedom of being me in the here and now.

God and you are one.
GOD IS ME sees you as your true self,
uncovered from beneath all your masks,
Free of all your prisons and attachments.
And in spite of your circumstances, GOD IS ME loves GOD IS YOU
Because I know who you truly are.
Just like me, you are one, and you are all.

---

91 The Gospel of Thomas 37:20–35 in Nag Hammadi Library 121.

God and we are one.
In my super consciousness,
Here is a vast space, like the clear night sky full of stars.
Each point of light in this vastness
is a concentration, a focus of consciousness, and a unique kind of knowing.
Each has a name: Mary Magdalene, Jesus, Buddha, Gandhi, Hiawatha.
With each, I can talk with as I would with a best friend.
I am as God is: ALL.
I am as God is: ONE.
Every rock,
Every tree,
Every planet,
Every star,
Every bug,
Every breeze,
Every fart,
Every sneeze.

✢✢

Chapter 8

Can Christians Be Saved?

Introduction

In 1517, Martin Luther nailed his 95 theses to the door of the All Saints Church in Wittenberg, which sparked the Protestant Reformation. One could say that the reform that was sparked by Luther saved Christianity. The Roman Catholic Church had become corrupt by offering indulgences, the forgiving of sins, in return for contributions of money. Luther's actions, along with the proliferation of printed Bibles made available to the common people due to the invention of moveable type and the printing press, helped the masses of people to be able to experience Christianity directly rather than through the intermediary of a priest or bishop. This was a very good thing. The only problem was that the Christianity typically experienced was literal Christianity.

Almost 500 years later, we now need another spiritual reformation. It is still possible for true Christianity to provide great hope to our world by returning to the mystical roots of its early centuries. As we have explained, this would involve releasing the dogma, rules, and regulations of the literal text and finding spiritual truth within, based upon the ancient stories and rituals represented by the Bible.

Much dogma needs to be released for Christianity to survive and remain as a spiritual foundation for our future. Listed below are a series of ideas that have grown through the years since the Council of Nicaea. These are the ideas that, we believe, keep Christianity and other major Western religions stuck in their current dualistic worldview. This view promotes separation, inhibits the experience of oneness, and promotes the continuation of wars.

Faith: This is often disguised as believing in handed-down dogma. Our faith can be handed down from our parents, friends, or our cultural beliefs. Faith can also mean believing in the validity of our own experiences. When these experiences are guided by the wisdom and lessons contained in sacred literature, such as the Christian Bible, we establish an inner faith in our own personal truth. This is what gives us freedom, leading to salvation and heaven on earth.

The God Position: God is not out there. There is no god in the heavens pondering our lives with omniscience. God is within us. As we acknowledge this truth, we can perform works of love and compassion to change our world.

Jesus is not to be worshiped as our Lord and master: Jesus became embodied to show us the way to God consciousness. He is our pattern of how to obtain enlightenment and experience God consciousness. We can worship all of Creation, including ourselves, with our respect, integrity, and honor. We worship others by esteeming them as one with us. We worship our world by taking care of it.

Heaven and Hell: Both of these states are in the here-and-now. As we create our lives, we can let the suffering that we encounter in this life either break us or inspire us. If the events of our world cause us to be broken by hating others or resenting our circumstances, then we experience hell. If we allow the events in our lives to mirror our internal loving consciousness, then we can live in heaven.

The Devil or Satan: This evil Christian god is none other than our own shadow side. We need not blame anything on the devil, for we must take responsibility for our lives and our well-being.

Sin: The church used this dualistic concept to control behavior and to demand obedience from its followers. Most of us in the West are programmed to judge. Often we judge ourselves most harshly and then label ourselves as sinners. We may also judge others as bad and needing punishment. As we live together with others in our world, a great universal rule would be to do no harm to anyone in any way. When we live in oneness, we find that we do not judge or punish others because that would be doing those things to ourselves.

Salvation is given to us in exchange for faith (or our belief): Obtaining salvation or enlightenment is considered as achieving the kingdom of heaven in this life, as Jesus taught. When we are led to believe that heaven is an after-death experience and the responsibility of Jesus, then we belittle ourselves by denying our inner divine selves. Furthermore, we are vulnerable to manipulation by church authorities. These authorities often succeed in convincing us that salvation is an escape from hell after death rather than a way of experiencing our lives in the present moment.

Suffering is part of the path to salvation: Contrary to the conventional belief, part of the path to salvation involves letting go of our suffering, our attachment to suffering, and our complicity in deepening our suffering. Bhagavan of the Oneness University teaches that anything fully experienced becomes joy. Our experiences with the allegories that we have described have proven this concept to us.

The Rev. Johnson[92] points out that God that was constructed as a male patriarchal god. During Biblical times, to spare themselves from God's wrath and vengeance, human beings projected all of their sins on innocent animals and slaughtered them. This Old Testament theology was carried over to the New Testament, in which Jesus became the sacrificial lamb or scapegoat. Projecting sins onto others, then sacrificing them, is a practice and a mindset that must be changed. Furthermore, Johnson points out that the paradigm has shifted somewhat: "It is not the shedding of innocent blood that supposedly appeases [God], but the shedding of guilty blood."

---

92 Rev. Deborah L. Johnson: Your Deepest Intent: Sounds True Inc., Boulder, CO 2007, pp 270-271

This sacrifice of guilty blood requires a basic belief in good and evil and the making of judgments.

Christian martyrs often wanted to suffer as Jesus had suffered by being tortured and sacrificed at the hands of the Romans. By suffering such a fate in actuality rather than symbolically, via a ritual, they missed the point of the allegory of death and resurrection and thus missed their entry into their imagined heaven.

Faith in exclusivity (believing that some are saved, while others are unsaved): Rita Gross, a Buddhist scholar, writes: "Exclusivist truth claims in religion, I would argue, are among the most dangerous, destructive, and immoral ideas that humans have ever created."[93] The idea that only one set of beliefs about God are right, while all others are wrong, is extremely troublesome for our world and continues today to produce terrible news almost daily. This idea further supports jihad and even has one sect of Muslims suicide bombing other sects, members of the Taliban torturing and killing women, and Pro-Life Christians murdering doctors who make legal abortions safe for the women who elect to have them.

Virginia Responds

The great truths of Christianity can be appropriated in our spirits through mysticism. Mysticism is the relationship and conscious awareness of God or divine consciousness by direct experience, intuition, or personal revelation. We have employed nondualistic mysticism in our processes and revelations in this book. Our beliefs are based not upon faith, but upon our personal experiences as we have come into union with divine consciousness or God. The mystical branches of all the Western religions are alike and confirm this truth, for example in Islam, the Sufi branch, and in Judaism, the Kabala branch.

---

93 Rita M. Gross: "This Buddhist's View of Jesus." *Buddhist-Christian Studies, 19.1* (1999) 62–75.

On a gay Christian forum, one of the members posted this comment in 2010:

> *"I see Christianity, for the most part, not encouraging its adherents to aspire to higher planes. I do not mean the heavenly afterlife. I mean higher planes of consciousness in this life. When I read The Book of Practicing the Way, by Lao-tzu, one of the most important texts of Chinese mysticism, I see it extolling the pursuit of inner virtue as a means to achieving a higher plane of existence."*

> —*anonymous blogger*

In practice, all churches train their followers in basically the same way. Thinking outside the box is not encouraged and may be even sanctioned. Questioning the faith and providing new interpretations of its scriptures or traditions are looked upon with suspicion. This has produced viewing Christian mysticism with suspicion. I have always incorporated elements of Buddhist philosophy into my beliefs. The premise that suffering in this life is caused by our attachments to possessions or ideas is found in the Four Noble Truths of Buddhism, but these can also be found in the Gospel of Matthew in sayings attributed to Jesus.[94]

Looking at each Biblical story allegorically and experiencing the stories internally in meditation or with Gestalt processes can lead one to higher states of consciousness. Doing so brings God inside us, where God belongs. This higher state of consciousness is accessible to all. Unfortunately, most modern-day Christians see little value in accessing higher consciousness through Christian pathways, yet I have found that it has led to a deepening of God consciousness and an appreciation of all of us on this planet.

The discoveries that we have made in internalizing Biblical stories do exactly what the member of the gay forum suggested. By seeing Jesus and God in a new light, we evolve as people with God

---

94 Matthew 6:24–34.

consciousness. During our work together, we mirrored and experienced the life of Jesus and what it could show us about how to live. We were born with him, and we learned and studied with him. We were baptized with him and tempted with him. We tried to teach the disciples with him, and then we were crucified and resurrected as him.

Jesus was born to Mary and Joseph. From the beginning of his life, he came to earth to show us all what being God is about. Initially, his training revolved around the elimination of his ego or rendering his ego irrelevant. Most of his dreams and visions centered on the salvation of the world. When it was time for Jesus to begin his public speaking and ministry, his cousin, John, who honored Jesus as the one way to bring us to God, baptized him. This was also how Jesus showed his commitment to live as the God of Love, not the God of Judgment and Anger. During the three years of his ministry, Jesus struggled with letting go of Jehovah and accepting the God of Love within him. During his Crucifixion (which can be seen as a ritual), he attained God realization when he said, "My God, why have you forsaken me?" He had fully given up and transcended the God of Judgment represented by the tree of the knowledge of good and evil. At the end of that ritual, he rose as the God of Love, the tree of life. He lived his life as a pattern and an example of the way to know God within oneself. That is why he said, "I am the way, the truth, and the life." He was and is a way to God realization. Jesus is our pattern to God realization.

—Virginia retells the story of Jesus

We know many Christians, and, as mentioned above, we were conservative Christians once upon a time. Our heart is truly for the blessing of each person who reads this book. We have offered this book as a gift to Christians. All of us want to know the truth of life and to find how to apply that truth to our lives. Jesus said, "I come that they might have life and live more abundantly." The truth must be helpful to us in our lives. The Bible should yield these deep truths that have been embedded in the literal text. It seems incredible that the truth of the mysteries is that we all are the God of this universe and part of the Divine.

If each of us is divine, then each of us is worthy of worship, and we should worship the Divine within ourselves and in each other, which is what is represented symbolically in the story of the pregnant Mary's visit to her pregnant kinswoman, who was carrying John the Baptist. The baby in her womb leapt for joy upon encountering Jesus, whom John would later baptize. Some call this respecting each other, but we call it worship. We can celebrate our lives together as we raise our voices of praise in a wonderful adoration of the human and the Divine being one. Jesus taught us to do this through his life, and the Gospels support this thesis. All that Jesus said about being God and "I am my Father are one" were statements of his oneness with God. Jesus continually encouraged others to follow him. Follow him? Where? "Into oneness with the God of Love." And when we follow the life of Jesus, as we have done, we can see that we can become one with God. The Gospel of John says, "For God so loved the world that he gave his only begotten son, that whosoever believes in him shall not perish, but shall have everlasting life."[95] This refers not to the sacrifice that Jesus made on the Cross, but to the fact that by his pattern, we could consider ourselves divine. Our intention upon death is not to die, but to continue.

Jesus said in the Sermon on the Mount not to worry about your life, your money, or the lack of it, not to worry about what you will wear or the roof over your head, but seek first the kingdom of God, and all these things will be provided for.[96] Has your faith enabled

95 John 3:16.
96 Matthew 6:25–34.

you to realize this blessing? We have realized this by our experience. We have seen that as we live our lives with the intention of blessing others, that contentment, peace, and power are present. This is the God Position.

There are many ways in which you can create such a life for yourself. One way we have found is to become givers of oneness blessings. Originating with Sri AmmaBhagavan at the Oneness University in India, a worldwide group of persons is spreading the oneness blessing across the world. The actual blessing is a one-minute intention of world awakening by placing our hands lightly upon the head of another person. This powerful intention has the resulting blessing of meeting the needs of the person being blessed, as well as speeding the world toward awakening. We have found this to be a wonderful way to be of service to others and to be blessed ourselves as we give the blessing.

There are many other ways you could become involved, whether they be through churches that teach oneness, such as Unity or Unitarian churches, or even many pagan groups that hold space for world awakening. Many of the Native spiritual philosophies teach oneness. There are many places on the Internet that could help you to connect to others who have embraced oneness. You may even contact either of us via the contact information found in the appendix.

Buck Speaks

I would like to save Christians from their belief that non-Christians are not saved and are going to hell. I would like to save Muslims from their belief that non-Muslims are infidels and are going to hell. I would like to save Jews from their belief that non-Jews are not chosen by God. I would like to grant a divorce to people from all of their ideas that create separation, and from their religious dogma. The Christianity that Jesus achieved through his ritual of death and resurrection can do this. He realized that he became Christ, the Son of the God of Love. He was no longer separate from anything in Creation.

A vast amount of literal Christian dogma or what is called faith is not love. It creates separation; it creates judgment. And it creates a justification for killings and wars. Because faith has been given such a sacred place in the minds of fundamentalists, it creates a mindset that is not allowed to wander outside this box called faith. Different religions and different denominations of the same religions have different approaches to faith, different sets of beliefs or dogma. How can the God of Love be the author of such rules? Can't Christians be saved from the separations created by all these made-up rules, from this dogma made sacred by calling it faith?

⁂

Chapter 9

Final Words

A Story of Jesus

With great care I have been observing the astrological signs and now I know both the time and place where this special child is to be born. I gather my two wise and beloved friends and we make the long journey to Judea. Mistakenly, we stop to ask advice from their King Herod. Fortunately he doesn't know of whom we are speaking; yet he shows intense signs of suspicion and jealousy.

Thanking him, we take our leave to avoid the king and his servants for the rest of our journey.

After a more careful examination of the signs we are able to be guided to just the right place. We find the new born child and his parents all well but a bit mystified. We instruct them with our knowing; we bless them with our love and the grace of the divine; and we give them gifts so that they will be able to move to Egypt and provide the child with both safety and the best education.

This boy proves to be an excellent student; actually he is at the top of his classes and excels in all his initiations. The family eventually returns to Judea after the old king has died. The boy is brought to study and live in the Essene community. Again he excels and passes through his initiations with great admiration.

Older now the boy sets out to visit the great centers of wisdom throughout the world. Fortunately, his parents and now he has been using our gifts carefully and wisely. He has the resources for these great journeys. He studies and takes initiations in many great schools and in many lands before returning to Judea.

He starts to teach as well as to prepare for his final initiation which he will have to manage alone. He starts this preparation by asking his surprised cousin, John to baptize him. This begins his final ritual. Not yet fully aware of the implications of all of his actions, he recruits twelve men as students or disciples as they came to be known.

Just before the last steps of the ceremony they eat together in what becomes known as the Last Supper. As his final act with them he offers a toast of his body, symbolized as the bread: saying to them: "Take this, my body, eat and become one with me." Then he offers them wine: saying to them: "Take this, my blood, and drink and become one with we." He further instructs them to often share bread and wine like this so that they will reinforce their understanding that they were one with each other. Eventually, they will come to understand that they were not only one with each other but one with all of creation and one with the divine that is within. By doing this they will be following in the path of Oneness with God as Jesus is now doing.

But as he observes them, he realizes that they are still not fully where he had hoped that they would be. He is saddened and frustrated.

He then surprises them by saying he is going to wash their feet. First they object, but then agree as he becomes insistent and gives them further teachings. He receives amazing realizations during this ritual. First, he realizes that to succeed in the final ceremony he must stand in for every human, not only those who are present with him now, but all humans throughout all of history and all future. And he must do this with the greatest of humility, truly feeling their pains and sufferings. He understands that if he can really do this then his pains and sufferings will also be absolved and converted into joy. Second he realizes, that over their time together each of his disciples has been mirroring back to him the way he gets out of balance. As he watches each of them, he is symbolically cleaning the mirror that they are to him: he really sees them and himself as one and understands what his life with them has been teaching him about himself. He, the teacher, becomes he who is being taught. Finally he sees his whole, complete and true self. He loves himself as who he truly is.

He needs to pray to strengthen his will so that he can face this last ceremony. He still feels disappointed because his students are still exhibiting their fallacies especially those who drank too much ceremonial wine. And so when Jesus prays, they are too sleepy to attend him. He now realizes a third lesson; he must face his fate totally alone. Not only must he experience the suffering of all humankind but he must experience his own suffering and still be able to accept himself as he is and love himself even when he is totally alone.

Finally, it is clear to him how to proceed. He allows himself to be arrested, accused, and sentenced to death. He will drag the cross upon which he is to hang through the city and up the hill of death. He will not let all the injuries and hurtful words deter him. He will allow himself to feel it all.

At the peak of the suffering he cries out: "My God, I am forsaking thee." By this act, he wills to break the bonds of duality symbolized by the God of the Old Testament and the Tree of the Knowledge of Good and Evil. By this act, he succeeds in making the great transition to becoming the Son of the God of Love.

For a few hundred years after Jesus became Christ, some of humankind, realized the significance of the example that Jesus set. His teachings were being accepted by people who called themselves Christians. At first the powerful leaders of Rome tried to stamp out this new and growing religion, but the more they tried, the more it grew. Finally, in a most cleaver political move, the Emperor of the Empire, Constantine, claimed Christianity his official religion. But even cleverer, they took the branch of Christianity that could best be used to control people and set out to support only the literalist Christian teachers and to destroy the true teachings of Jesus. They kill or banish all Christian teachers who didn't agree with them and destroy their writings. Furthermore they made Jesus God, an external god that people would be forced to worship and obey like they were forced to worship and obey the Emperor. This was O.K. for Rome because the living Emperor of Rome controlled the definition of this absent God. For two thousand years, the real teachings were buried in the sand or caves. But now they have been revealed again. I wonder if any of humankind will actually notice.

—The Wise Man with the gold
speaking through Buck

Buck Speaks

It's the day we expect to receive back the fully edited manuscript, yet here comes two more messages, one from the wise man (given above) who visited the newborn Jesus and one from Gurubhai.

Today, as Gurubhai and I sat in the garden for our usual early morning meditation, Gurubhai plays his drums and sings as he often does. He, like the first Skih Guru, Nanak, is able to allow a song to simply roll out of his mouth. As he starts playing and then begins to spontaneously create, he is singing about the twelve disciples of Jesus. Not only is the song most enjoyable, but to my great delight, the words of his song integrates that which we have been learning together about the symbolic meaning of each of the disciples. These are the lessons Jesus got in the foot washing ritual, but furthermore apply to our individual lives. He sings. I listen; afterwards we recall the message of the song. His song today was an appreciation of what the disciples mirror to us of the best qualities of their/our personalities. Unfortunately, I don't remember the poetic words he sang but later we were able to match up the best of each disciple with what each of them individually reflected back to Jesus and now reflect back to us.

Peter, the Aries — Divinely inspired leadership
John the Leo — Unconditional love
James the Sagittarius — Powerful will to walk righteously
Simon the Taurus — Speaking divine revelations
Phillip the Virgo — Eating and drinking in the divine
Matthew the Capricorn — Walking with the divine
James the Gemini — Serving with grace and love
Nathaniel the Libra — Harmonizing and making music
Thaddeus the Aquarian — Knowing how to walk the divine pathway
Andrew the Cancer — Welcoming and nurturing
Thomas the Scorpio — Surrendering doubts and passion for the divine,
Judas the Pisces — Returning to Oneness

—Gurubhai Khalsa

A Prayer for the Reader

Our prayer for you, dear reader, is that you will have the experiences in your life that will lead you to fully know your true self and to realize that you are one with the Divine: your vision of the Divine is as your truest, dearest, and most trusted inner friend. Our prayer is to bless you in your being you, in your knowing you, and in your loving yourself. May this knowing and loving extend to your family, your friends, and to all others. May you find and live in peace and dwell within your very own heaven on earth. May you be free from all separations, allowing yourself to hang out in the joy of being who you are. May you have faith in your beliefs that are derived from the experiences that you have truly lived. And may you live amongst others who, like you, have found their true selves. For blessed are those who know and love themselves.

✳✳✳

Appendix I

Contact Information

Virginia T. Stephenson: witast@aol.ocm

Buck A. Rhodes: BuckRhodes@aol.com

Blog: www.canchristiansbesaved.com

Oneness University: www.onenessuniversity.org

World Oneness Community: www.worldonenesscommunity.com

More information on transgender spirituality: www.Transspirit council.org

✳✳

Appendix 2

Teaching Oneness from Other Mystic Traditions

The concept of oneness has long been appreciated in the mystic traditions of Western religions other than Christianity. Two major examples of this are Kabalistic Cross from Kabalistic studies, which originated in Judaism, and a Sufi Zikr, which originated in Islam.

Currently, the Kabalistic Cross is utilized in Golden Dawn Temple magic to establish a sacred space at the beginning of ceremonies.[97] This version has been expanded to emphasis its use as an affirmation for oneness.

Kabalistic Cross

The Kabalistic Cross is called out while standing, facing the east.

(I)   The right hand is raised above the head and moves downward infront of the body while saying in a commanding voice: *"ATEH."*

---

97 Isreal Regardie: *The Golden Dawn* (St. Paul, MN: Llewellyn, 1937).

(2) The right hand is extended towards the floor while saying: "*MALKUTH.*"

(3) The right hand is extended outwards from the body and moved from this extension back to the chest while saying: "*VE-GEBURAH.*"

(4) The right hand is extended towards the left of the body and moved from this extension back to the chest while saying: "*VE-GEDULAH.*"

(5) The right hand traces a circle around the heart while saying: "*LE-OLAM.*"

(6) Both hands are brought to the prayer position while saying: "*AMEN.*" [98]

To state the corresponding affirmations of oneness, the words given on the following page are also recited. For example, after saying AHEH and making the first hand movement, say: "I am God; I am Goddess. I am wholly within the Divine and one with all of Creation. I am existence, consciousness, and bliss."

Affirmation of Oneness Based on The Tree of Life [99]

ATEH
I am God; I am Goddess.
I am wholly within the Divine
And one with all of Creation.
I am existence, consciousness, bliss.

---

98 Notice: You have drawn a cross on your body with a circle round the intersection of the two cross members. This is the Kabalistic Cross.

99 The first line of each stanza is the original version; the following lines have been added through years of repeated usage.

MALKUTH
I am Man; I am Woman.
I am both rational and emotional,
Using both my intellect and my intuition.
I am existence, consciousness, bliss.

VE-GEBURAH, VE-GEDULAH
I am a saint; I am Satan.
I am severity; I am kindness.
I am the whole and the truth of every story,
The darkness, as well as the light.
I am existence, consciousness, bliss.

LE-OLAM
Now I ride the wave of time/space.
For I am forever,
Connecting the past to the future.
I am existence, consciousness, bliss.

AMEN
I am oneness
And the end of duality.
I am existence, consciousness, bliss.

Zikr[100]

Round I
Al Elaha El Elahu. (Nothing exists. Only God exists.)

When Thou didst sit upon Thy throne, with a crown upon Thy head, I did prostrate myself upon the ground and called Thee my Lord.

Round 2
El Elahu. (Only God exists.)

When Thou didst stretch out Thy hands in blessing over me, I knelt and called Thee my Master.

Round 3
Allahu. (God is unity)

When Thou dist raise me from the ground, holding me with Thine arms, I drew closer to Thee and called Thee my Beloved.

Round 4
Hu. (Om.)

But when Thy caressing hands held my head next to Thy glowing heart and Thou didst kiss me, I smiled and called Thee myself.

✳✳

---

100   This comes from the Sufi tradition and was given to me by a friend, along with a recording of the music that goes with this. Each round is chanted for several minutes while sitting and moving the head and upper body in a circle to the rhythm of the music. When done sincerely, the experience of being one with the Divine is profound.

Appendix 3

Chakra Dhyana

This is reportedly a 5000 years Indian practice to raise the kundalini energy and is often used prior to giving and receiving deeksha or Oneness blessings.

Chakra Color Balance the Extremes of: Chant x 7

Chorus: after each Chakra, chant: **Kundalini Aro hanam** x 5

---

1   <u>Root</u>: Teaching: *Suffering is not in the fact, but in your perception of the fact.*

    Red   Certainty and Uncertainty   **Lang**

---

2   <u>Genitals</u>: Teaching: *The world is a mirror. The situations you experience in the world outside are a reflection of your inner state of consciousness.*

    Orange   Indulgence and Abstinence   **Vang**

---

3   <u>Power</u>: Teaching: *Anything when experienced fully becomes joy.*

Yellow   Dominance and Subservience   **Rang**

4   <u>Heart</u>: Teaching: *To love is to accept yourself as you are.*

Green   Possessiveness and Indifference   **Yang**

5   <u>Throat</u>: Teaching: *If you recognize that divine grace flows into your life as coincidences, you rise in love and gratitude.*

Blue   Resignation and Extreme Seeking **Hang**

6   <u>Third Eye</u>: Teaching: *The inner journey begins with an awareness of where you are, not with an obsession with where you want to be.*

Indigo   Carelessness and Perfection   **AaaaaaOoooMm**

7   <u>Crown</u>: Teaching: *Freedom is not in the transformation of content, but in experiencing it as it is.*

Magenta   Analysis and Synthesis   **Ogum Satyam Om**

✡✡

Appendix 4

The Descent of Inanna[101]

Enki the Wise is the god of fresh water and wisdom. He is a great helper of humankind and gave to us the Seven Sages, who taught us many arts and skills. To the beautiful Inanna, of whom he is most fond, he gave many gifts as well: wisdom, justice, love, the sacred women, and the fruit of the vine. Inanna is the morning star and the evening star, the rose, and Queen of the Heavens. She is the daughter of Sen, the god of the moon.

Inanna has a sister named Ereshkigal, who lives and rules in Irkalla, the land of the dead. Although Inanna was always very wise, in her youth, she knew nothing of her sister's land, but wanted to learn of it. She asked the permission of the other gods to go. After much hesitation and debate, they granted her wish.

So it was that Inanna went to the gates of Irkalla and petitioned the gatekeeper for entry. Actually, being in the fire of her youth and after all a goddess, she got pretty pushy about it. She said, "Here, gatekeeper: open your gate! If you don't open up, I'll smash the door

---

101 This version has been edited, but was originally taken from:
http://www.philomuse.com/jsk/vp_archive/lab/descent.htm VTS

and shatter the bolt! I'll raise up all the dead, and they shall come up to earth and eat the living, until there's more dead than alive!" Well, that certainly got the gatekeeper's attention. He got on the horn to Ereshkigal right away.

Needless to say, Ereshkigal was not amused. "What does *she* want?" Ereshkigal hissed. "For bread I eat clay, for beer I drink muddy water. It is I who must weep for the young men taken from their sweethearts, for the young girls taken from their lovers' laps. It is I who must weep for the infants taken so long before their time. Does she want a piece of that? Or is it the Water of Life she wants?" For it was true that Ereshkigal did keep the Water of Life down there, a most prized possession in such a bleak place. "Go ahead, gatekeeper, and let her in. But treat her to the ancient rites, as all must endure on their way to me."

Back up top, the gatekeeper smiled feebly and unlocked the gate. "Enter, my lady. May you find joy here. May Irkalla be happy to see you." At that he snatched Inanna's great crown.

Inanna roared in anger. "Return my crown! Who are you to remove the crown of a goddess?"

"Go forth, my lady," answered the gatekeeper solemnly. "Such are the ancient rites."

Soon they came to another gate. The gatekeeper unlocked it, and as Inanna passed through, he removed her earrings.

"Why have you taken my earrings?" Inanna demanded to know, a little less indignant this time.

"Such are the ancient rites, my lady," said the gatekeeper. And this went on for several more gates, seven in all. The gatekeeper took her necklace, then her breast pins, her girdle of birthstones, the bangles on her wrists and ankles, and at last her very gown. Finally, after passing through the seventh gate, Inanna found herself standing naked before Ereshkigal.

Ereshkigal had expected Inanna to be frightened and contrite by this point, and although Inanna was a bit flustered, you would have never known it. Indeed, it was Ereshkigal who was trembling, for although Inanna had been stripped of all of her finery, her radiant presence was overwhelming in the dark, musty palace. Ereshkigal motioned to her vizier. "Namtar!" she cried. "Send out against her the sixty diseases!"

Now Inanna is tough, but sixty diseases from the Queen of the Dead is enough to slow anybody down. Inanna fell to the ground, and Ereshkigal threw Inanna into a lampless cell to die.

Meanwhile, back on earth, the people and the animals were beginning to miss Inanna. Without their beautiful goddess of love, the people fell into despair. The animals in the forests and fields despaired too. Even the bees and butterflies stopped pollinating. The world plunged into a terrible winter, and famine began to ravage the land. Finally Papsukkal, Inanna's brother, went to their father the moon god and told him of the tragedies befalling the earth. Together, they went to see Enki the Wise.

Enki the Wise devised a plan. He created a being to save Inanna and to be her close and trusted friend. From the dirt beneath his fingernails he made Asushunamir, whose name means "he/she whose face is brilliant." And being luminescent like the moon, Asushunamir passed directly into the underworld from the overworld, as only the moon can do. In the dark palace of the underworld, she appeared before Ereshkigal.

"Oh, my my, what have we here?" Ereshkigal cried. She was overtaken with desire at his/her beauty and became immediately obsessed with taking Asushunamir to her bed. She called for a lavish feast in his/her honor and had her best wine brought to the table. Asushunamir sang in an ethereal voice for Ereshkigal and danced sensually, but was careful not to eat any food prepared by ghosts and to pour her wine on the floor when Ereshkigal wasn't looking.

When Ereshkigal had at last become very drunk, Asushunamir asked of her, "Oh great and lovely queen, is it not true you keep the Water of Life here? For I have heard it is so, and I have longed to taste it."

"Namtar!" Ereshkigal cried. "Bring me the jug that holds the Water of Life! I shall grant this magnificent creature's wish."

When Ereshkigal finally passed out in a drunken stupor, Asushunamir quietly took the jug to the cell where Inanna lay dying. Asushunamir sprinkled the Water of Life upon Inanna, and she quickly began to revive, her eyes regaining their sparkle and her face flushing pink like a child's. Hurriedly she rose, and bidding Asushunamir to follow, raced upward through the seven gates and back to earth. As she burst through the final door, the flowers immediately began to open and the grass to become green, as the skies cleared at last.

Asushunamir was not so fortunate. Just as Asushunamir was approaching the seventh gate, Ereshkigal awakened, and no amount of music, dance, or flattery could charm her now.

"The food of the gutter shall be your food!" Ereshkigal shrieked. "The drink of the sewer shall be your drink! In the shadows you shall abide."

When Inanna learned of the curse placed upon her friend, she wept and spoke softly to her. "The power of Ereshkigal is great," she said. "Even I cannot break her spell. But I may soften her curse upon you.

"For many ages, you will suffer. Those who are like you, my assinnu, kalum, kurgarru, and kalaturru, lovers of men, kin to my sacred women, shall be strangers in their own homes. Their families will keep them in the shadows and will leave them nothing. The drunken shall smite their faces, and the mighty shall imprison them.

"But if you will remember me, how you were born from the light of the stars to save me from death, to rid the Earth of winter, then I shall harbor you and your kind. I shall give you the gift of prophecy, the wisdom of the earth and moon. You shall banish illness from my children, as you healed me in Irkalla. And when you robe yourself in my robes, I shall dance in your feet and sing in your throats. And no man shall be able to resist your enchantments.

"When the Water of Life is brought up from Irkalla, then lions shall leap in the deserts, and you shall be freed from the spell of Ereshkigal. Once more, you shall be called Asushunamir, the Shining Ones, Those Who Have Come to Renew the Light, the Blessed Ones of Inanna."[102]

---

102 This myth is from the Sumerian civilization, circa 2000 BCE.

Reflections on the Myth
By Virginia Stephenson

This is an introduction to the ritual written from inspiration from the Descent of Inanna. The ritual is given in the chapter on initiations.

The Myth of the Descent of Inanna is full of symbolism and allegory, which can be reflective of many spiritual paths. The story has been used in Wiccan and pagan ritual and ceremony, as well as other spiritual walks. It obviously can show us much wisdom for all people, but I have chosen to discuss how the myth can apply and be used by transgender people reclaiming those ancient places of service and honor. Although the following discussion explores only that particular application, it serves as a model of how to claim an ancient myth and reclaim it to serve our needs today.

Inanna progressing through the seven gates to the Land of the dead, and having to give up all that she possessed, and standing at the gates naked, is exactly what gender transition looks like to the trans-gender person. We look at losing most things in our lives because of the oppression of the culture: job, home, family, friends, and even reputation. Those of us who have a spiritual path use this time for reflection on, among other things, the following questions: What is important to us in this life? What is our true nature? For some of us, losing these things is a time to detach from these them and let go of our fear of losing them. Many times, this is a life-changing event of being enlightened about who we are and what is important to us. As we stand in our truth, we are empowered by our courage. Some of us recognize that if we can go against the rules of something so basic to our culture as gender, then all things are possible to us. We give up our place in the male tribe, and we may take a place in the female tribe or in a third gender tribe. We stand naked ready for new clothes.

Some of us find great persecution, danger, and torment during and after the gender transition. Others of us pass through relatively unscathed. But we all have to stare fear in the eyes and move through that fear to our actualized self. It is an initiation, a proving, and a testing all in one. The wise among us use this precious time to seek truth in the world and inside us.

Asushunamir is the heroic character in the story. Created male and female, she is a type of all male-to-female transgender people as she goes into the land of the dead to rescue Inanna. It is said that she has a face that is "brilliant," and when Ereshkigal sees her, she immediately is enchanted and wants to have sex with her. Asushunamir prudently plays upon Ereshkigal's desire to trick Ereshkigal and save Inanna. As trans people, we need to realize that internalized trans-phobia must be defeated in our lives for us to live authentically. We can do anything we choose, and we can perform great feats and save people in this world. Those who are wise desire us, for we have exotic bodies and open minds, and our rich history of experiences can bring much wisdom to those who seek us out. Some of us have painful sexual histories, and others of us have given up on sexuality because we have deemed it too hard. We need to drink the water of life and be healed in every area of our lives. We must lay down the notion that we are scarred by our differentness and realize that our trans-nature has given to us precious gifts by which we can change our world.

We have chosen to change our bodies. For some, this is hormonal, while others opt for various surgeries to change the shape, outline, and looks of our bodies. We participate in cutting, stretching, folding, expanding, and reducing our flesh. This body modification comes as an intuitive decision, not a rational one. We know that we must change our bodies, and we do it as a result of feelings, hopes, and dreams, not because of rational input from the culture. Indeed, many of our friends and family have counseled us not to have these things done, yet we honored our intuition in this regard anyway. Knowing this truth for us, we then moved in rational ways to achieve our goals.

Similarly, much shamanic work and spiritual work is based on intuition, not rationality. Shamans look to an unseen world and journey to unseen lands to obtain wisdom, knowledge, prophecy, or healing for our clients or the world. Shamans sense how to bring wisdom and healing to people, based on our intuition. Transgender people are gifted with this knowledge of the intuitive by walking through the spiritual work of transition. For many of us, transition is a great life challenge. Our culture resists us and tries to apply severe sanctions on those who cross genders.

The curse by Ereshkigal on Asushunamir has come to pass on many transgender people. "For many ages, you will suffer. You and those like you . . . shall be strangers in their own homes. Their families will keep them in the shadows and will leave them nothing. The drunken shall smite their faces, and the mighty shall imprison them." For too long, we have endured despite this curse, which is supported by this culture, but now it is time to accept the blessing of Inanna:

> *"But if you will remember me, how you were born from the light of the stars to save me from death, to rid the earth of winter, then I shall harbor you and your kind. I shall give you the gift of prophecy, the wisdom of the earth and moon. You shall banish illness from my children, as you healed me in Irkalla. And when you robe yourself in my robes, I shall dance in your feet and sing in your throats. And no man shall be able to resist your enchantments."*
>
> —*Inanna*

This blessing speaks of the shamanic gifts to prophesy, to have wisdom, to be healers, to dance and sing in ritual, and to be attractive beings sought after for sex and romance, as well as for healing and wisdom. Indeed, in the unity of the genders can also be found the unity of sexuality and spirit, not only for setting intention in sacred space, but also for reaching ecstatic heights for personal connection or shamanic journeying.

The second part of the blessing speaks to future spiritual awakening:

> *"When the Water of Life is brought up from Irkalla, then lions shall leap in the deserts, and you shall be freed from the spell of Ereshkigal. Once more,*

you shall be called Asushunamir, the Shining Ones, Those Who Have Come to Renew the Light, the Blessed Ones of Inanna."

Our charge is to renew the light, even before we are free. Indeed, it is partly oppression that gives us great personal power, as we break its power by our intentions in our spiritual work. As we do this time and time again, we gain confidence to see the unseen and to see the unseen manifest itself in our lives. It is time for us to shine. It is time for us to take our place in the ancient places where we can help the world.

I see a ritual for transgender people arising from this myth. It can be a ritual used at gender transition or for a spiritual initiation, at a time when a trans person sees this new life and wishes to affirm that path and even to enter a spiritual path. The ritual can have three parts. The first is to take off all that is unnecessary—all emotional, psychological, painful events in the past, all fears and hurts—and lay them down and stand naked with nothing. The second part can be drinking the Water of Life and letting this pure wisdom and nourishment add compassion, love, forgiveness, integrity, confidence, and courage, as well as the gift of healing for us. The third part is receiving the blessings. As elders facilitate this, we can use foreknowledge and second sight to help them in what to take off. In the second part, we can intuit what the Water of Life means to them. In the third part, we can pronounce the blessing and add prophecy.

The ones to accept and do this ritual will be very blessed, and will feel that this solidifies their sense of belonging to the community.

✡✡

Appendix 5

Helping Others Analyze Their Dreams[103]

Buck A. Rhodes

Everything in your dream is a part of you and your inner world; the parts of the dream are bits and pieces of your psychic makeup. If your mother is in your dreams, then your subconscious facsimile of your mother is a part of who you are. This dream mother, although she may look like your mother, is not the same as your real mother in waking life; she is your internal-world mother. When you dream of your mother, your subconscious is inviting you to get to know this inner mother better. The better you know your internalized mother, the better you know your own self. This additional knowledge is often useful for improving your relationship with your real-world mother. This principle applies to every single thing in your dreams, including people, animals, things, ideas, and beliefs.

Now if you dream of a cow, what does this cow symbolize to you? What piece of your psyche is trying to get into your consciousness? The inner symbol *cow* can mean something entirely different to almost everybody; certainly, an American cowboy's cow is different from a Hindu's cow. If you were chased by a cow as a child, then what the cow symbolizes to you may be quite different. Thus if a dream expert assigns a generalized meaning to your dream cow, there may be some truth in that meaning, but there may be none. To know the true meaning of your own dream cow, you need to get your answer from your very own subconscious. The following method teaches you how to help someone actually discover what his or her various dream images actually mean to that individual and how they fit together.

This method comes from Fritz Perl's Gestalt therapy, modified by my study of Alchemical Hypnotherapy and years of facilitating others in the interpretation of their own dreams. The advantage is that you, as the person who is helping someone else, do *not* have to figure out the meaning of that person's dream. The dreamer will do this for himself or herself during the process. So then, just what do you do? You listen. You listen to what the person says and does not say. You guide, and you ask questions. This process usually takes about an hour.

To help someone understand a dream, select a quiet place where you can work undisturbed for an hour or more. During the process, the one with the dream will often go into a light hypnotic trance. This is not necessary, but is usually helpful. And you may want to end the process by helping the person to get back into ordinary reality.

This is how it works. Ask your friend to tell you the dream in the present tense. Using the present tense is very important. Interrupt whenever the person starts to use the past tense and ask him or her to restate what was just said in the present tense. You should make note of the things that are mentioned and note those that you feel are significant. You also can take notice of things that seem to be passed over quickly or avoided. When the person gets to the end of the dream, you immediately have the person start over, again using the present tense. The person needs to tell you the dream three times in this manner. This process gives the time needed to get back into the dream fully. Often by this time, the person recalling the dream is in a light trance. After the third telling or retelling, the two of you are ready to start to work to find the dream's meaning.

But before going into this next process, let's describe what you may discover by listening to and writing notes about the dream. You can notice the important things (symbols), such as the persons or characters who are mentioned or objects that get your attention (for example, an overturned wedding cake). I often underline or star key symbols—both obvious and subtle. For example, once in a dream about a family wedding, the dreamer barely mentioned seeing her mother across the room in only one of three initial tellings of the dream. Given that a mother is usually a very important part of a wedding, and as she was barely mentioned only once, I became alert to fact that the mother was minimized. Thus, I became suspicious that she was a key dream symbol, however subtle. Other key symbols were obvious, including the bride and groom. Another key symbol was the setting of the dream—in this case, the wedding reception room where most of the dream took place. The setting was the container for this dream and thus contained the different parts of the dream, that is, different parts of the psyche presented in the dream.

Sometimes important symbols don't actually show up in the dream. For example, the friend getting ready to tell me her dream mentioned more than once a tarot reading in which a particular card was very significant. Although she didn't mention the card in her dream, it turned out to be highly significant to her dream's interpretation. The dream, as it turned out, was her psyche's interpretation of this card as it represented her current life situation—the subject of a recent tarot card reading.

Now back to the actual process. After the third telling of the dream and the identification of the key symbols involved, you ask the dreamer to become one of the symbols and then tell the dream as this symbol, such as the bride in the wedding dream. You might start by saying: "Now become the bride and tell me the dream as you imagine the dream was for you (the bride). Again, tell the dream in the present tense." (Using the present tense should be easy by now.) After the dream telling, in this case by the bride, you may want to ask some follow-up questions. For example: "How do you know (so-in-so—someone in the dream)?" Or: "Do you have anything you want to say to (someone who appeared in the dream)?" Or even: "What do you see as important in this dream?" The last question may be: "Is there anything else that you want to mention?" When you feel complete with the information from this symbol, then you can move onto the next one. Do this by thanking the imagined person and asking whether you can call that person or character back if further questions arise. I often do the important characters first and then switch to other things, such as the overturned wedding cake in the previous example.

You repeat this process with various characters and objects identified in the previous tellings. As you keep going through the dream, you will likely notice that the dreamer is becoming clearer about the meaning of the dream. But you may want to ask: "Is there anyone else in the dream that needs to speak?" And often there is, so you invite this additional character or object to tell the dream. In a recent case, the dreamer replied that the higher self of one of characters wanted to speak. This character's comments provided extremely valuable insights into the dream. Interestingly, the higher self was of a person who didn't actually ever appear in the original dream. The dream started with the dreamer moving into a new house in which clothing had been left in the closet by the previous owner. The prior owner seemed to me to be one of these subtle symbols, so I asked that the dream be told by this character. This previous owner had a very interesting story to tell. While she was moving out, her child died. She was too upset to go back into the house to get her clothes; in fact, she never wanted to see her old clothes again.

Finally, when the dream has been retold by the various significant parts or symbols, you ask the dreamer to become the container of the dream. In the example above, this was the room where the wedding reception was held. You then say something like this: "Now you (the reception room) have contained most of the parts of the dream, so will you tell (the dreamer) why she had this particular dream and why now?" Sometimes, one of the characters will explain the dream to the dreamer. In the case of the significant tarot card, the card was given voice and actually provided the explanation.

After the initial three tellings of the dream, the dreamer will usually have no trouble in becoming the parts of the dream that you suggest. Sometimes, it helps to say to the dreamer: "Now take a deep breath and allow yourself to become . . ." Sometimes the dreamer may realize which of the symbols are important and need to tell the dream from that symbol's point of view. The understanding of the dream comes from the Gestalt or the overall composite from hearing and seeing the several points of view of the dream by the various characters and objects of the dream. The Gestalt or big understanding is often best expressed by the container or by one of the characters or other symbols. For example, in one dream, there was an old man who was selling strange magical toys. The dreamer had spoken to the old man in a harsh way. But it turned out that this character had several important things to relay to the dreamer that really helped her to understand the meaning of her dream.

It's good to ask the dreamer whether there is anything else that needs to be done before concluding with the analysis. If the dreamer feels complete, you may gently bring the dreamer back by counting up as when bringing a hypnotized person back to ordinary reality. Don't rush the dreamer back. A glass of water is often welcome at the conclusion of the analysis.

During the dream analysis, back-and-forth conversations between the dreamer and a character may prove valuable. This is done after asking the dreamer to become the character or symbol and telling the dream from that point of view. You may realize that a conversation between the two would be helpful. Ask the character to take a deep breath and become (the dreamer) again and invite them to ask any questions that they might have. After the question is asked, then you ask them to take a deep breath and become the character again. Continue the role reversal until the exchange is complete. You can ask both parties if they feel complete or say: "Let me know when you feel complete."

As you help people again and again, this process becomes easier and is almost always very interesting to both you and the person whom you are helping. This process builds an intimate relationship between the two of you. It is important to respect the confidentiality of the person who is sharing a dream with you. One big advantage of sharing a dream is that recurrent bad dreams are usually eliminated once the dream's message is understood by the dreamer. Sometimes, the person may become emotional during the analysis, but I've never seen anyone get anything from the analysis except relief and self-understanding. Sometimes, the process even provides great entertainment.

The steps of the process of dream analysis are outlined below.

OUTLINE OF

DREAM ANALYSIS

1. Tell the dream in the present tense three times.

2. Note what stands out and what may be hidden.

3. Identify the likely container of the dream.

4. Retell the dream as the different parts.

5. Ask questions of the part and/or initiate a dialogue between the part and the dreamer.

6. Ask the container to explain to the dreamer the meaning of the dream and why the dream was given.

7. Invite the dreamer to return to ordinary reality.

When parts of ourselves have been hidden and ignored, yet are important for us to know who we are, they are likely to appear symbolically in a dream. Keeping these parts in the closet serves as a defense mechanism: "Ignorance is bliss!" But our subconscious, desiring relief from the efforts of keeping something hidden, is likely to invite us to observe this part of ourselves that we are trying to avoid or ignore by presenting it symbolically to us in a dream. So when we give these hidden parts a voice, what we hear may not be all that comfortable; in fact, these parts may sometimes make us uncomfortable. Thus it is important to realize that dream analysis, although very useful, can be stressful. Thus you who are helping someone understand a dream need to be supportive and comforting to the dreamer. The dreamer is wise to approach this process with the intention of making his or her life better and a willingness to go through the internal muck to accomplish this. Fortunately, the ah-ha gotten from a well-understood dream makes the process worthwhile.

Being in the Present Moment

When you are helping someone to analyze a dream, your first task is to help the person get into the present moment of the dream. One of Fritz Perls' great teachings was to facilitate being in the present moment.[104] Thus the dreamer needs to return to the dream or to bring the dream forward into the present moment, where the dream again becomes alive and active. As the dreamer (or dream teller) is now awake, the dream comes under this person's conscious control, and your job is to help him or her to control the dream as it unfolds again and again under the scrutiny of you both. The dream teller needs to relive the dream in the present moment, and this happens because you won't allow the dream teller to use any past tenses. If the dream teller does, you immediately stop and ask the dream teller to repeat what was just said, but in the present tense. At times, you may have to coach the dream teller, for example, by saying: "Say it this way; 'I see . . .' " (rather than "I saw"). Don't let the dream teller get into an analytical mode; if the dream teller says: "I thought, or I don't remember," have him or her say: "In the dream, I notice . . ." If something important has been forgotten, it will likely come up during a repeat telling of the dream. Things that don't surface are usually unimportant. Having a good and complete memory of the dream is <u>not</u> nearly as important as getting into the dream and letting it unfold in the current moment.

Let yourself be in the dream teller's dream—as when you are watching a good movie, not only are you watching it, but also you are *in it*. When you are watching a movie, but don't get *in it*, the show gets boring, and you lose interest in it. So simply allow yourself to visualize what the dream teller is relating—visualize it as if it were happening right now.

For example, you may suggest to the dreamer that he or she should become the room (or place) in the dream, suggesting that the dream teller should say: "I am this room" and suggest describing self

---

104   www.here-be-dreams.com/psychology/perls.html "A major goal of Gestalt work is to live fully in the present and in doing so to gain insight into ourselves and hence stimulate growth."

just as the particular room in the dream. It is important, even if the room actually exists externally (in the waking world) not to attempt a description of the external room, but to stay within the room as it appears or feels or is experienced in the dream. As you listen to the description, you, too, can imagine yourself in this room. This can be a very dramatic and emotional because you both become consciously involved in the immense realms of experience hidden within the image. You are sharing the dream as you would share a movie with a fellow moviegoer.

Sometimes it may feel important to ask the dream teller: "What are you feeling at the present moment?" This can help to make sure that the dream teller is experiencing the present moment of the dream emotionally, as well as visually, during the retelling. However, it is usually unnecessary to interrupt the telling of a dream because an interruption might bring the dream teller out of the dream.

Helping someone analyze a dream requires a relaxed attitude on your part. It is like taking a walk with someone and sharing back and forth with the person what is going on in the present moment.

"When we are awake, we say that we had a dream, but when we are dreaming, we know that the dream has us."[105] Thus both you and the one whom you are helping need to let the current dream *have you* as it comes from the dream teller's mouth.

What Stands Out, What's Hidden, and What Contains the Dream

As the helper, you are a detective; you are looking for clues. You are an archeologist looking for hidden or obscure, but meaningful, artifacts. You ask yourself: "What in the story has a message for the dreamer?" For example, in the dream about the new house with clothes left behind by the previous owner that were still in the closet, I got a hit of curiosity about the person who left their clothes

---

105   http://improverse.com/ed-articles/**richard_wilkerson**_2003_aug_archetypal_psy-chology.htm

behind when moving. Now the dreamer is focused on the experience of her confusion as to why these clothes are in her new closet and the contrast between this puzzle and the excitement of having an otherwise clean and beautiful new house. Later, I asked the dreamer to become this previous homeowner and to tell the dream as this person's perspective.

Another time, a person dreamed that he had a new head, a head that had been grafted onto his neck. It was the head of a teenage boy. In the telling of the dream, he was delighted with his new, young, handsome head and enjoying feeling youthful. Also, he felt a big concern for the boy who had given up his head. My attention, while listening to this, was drawn to the seam between the old body and the new head. I would later ask the dream teller to become this seam and tell the dream from the seam's perspective. It turned out that this seam proclaimed that it was the boundary between his conscious and subconscious and that he really didn't have a new head. And the boy's head was his new self (subconscious), while the old body was his older self (or conscious self)—the dream was about a transition (renewal) that he is currently undergoing. The seam turned out to be a key clue to the meaning of the dream. When talking as the seam, the dream teller mentioned his thyroid gland. Later, when I asked him to become the thyroid, it was revealed that the thyroid was a group of organs that were hosting "pain bodies"[106] or pains programmed into him by his heritage and his ancestors. This led him to the realization that he would follow up this session with a ritual to burn and get rid of these pain bodies on behalf of both himself and his ancestors. This ritual seemed to be required for him to be free to manifest his newer, younger self without these old pains.

The rest of the body below the seam line in the dream represented the dreamer's older self. This was the part of him that was not free, but lived to meet the demands of his friends and family, an old self that felt imprisoned and laden with the pain bodies inherited from his ancestors.

---

106   Eckhart Tolle: "The Pain Body" (Chapter 5 in *A New Earth*, New York, NY: Dutton, Penguin Group, 2005).

In different example, the dreamer was in a field upon which it was raining happy, playful seals. The dreamer himself recognized these as an important symbol, which turned out to be a message to him from his subconscious that he needed to live a more playful life.

I estimate that typically, a dream teller will recognize at least half of the key dream symbols, while you will need to point out others to the dream teller. Sometimes, when I've suggested to the dream teller to become a certain character or part of the dream, the dream teller may respond, "I think that it would be better to do (so and so or such and such) next." I always go along with such a suggestion. Usually, I conclude by asking whether any other part of the dream has something to say.

The container of the dream is what puts it all together. Often, this is the setting: a house, a room, a field, etc. But just as likely, it may be a character in the dream. In the first section, it was pointed out that the old man selling magical trinkets was key to the synthesis of the dream. He represented a critical aspect of the dreamer that questioned some of her motives behind her activities, providing useful insights that her conscious mind had been avoiding. Incorporating these insights into her conscious life brought about some healthy changes in some of her ongoing activities.

In a dream with a clock and that expands a period of time, the clock might be the object to best explain the dream to the dreamer. Or if the dream setting is in a car, then this may be container. Also, it might be the higher self of the dreamer or a spiritual guide, especially if these happened to be mentioned during or before the telling of the dream.

Another option[107] in Gestalt dream work is to formulate an *existential statement*. An existential statement summarizes a basic theme in the dream that is also an important theme in the dreamer's waking life. For example: "I'm falling through the air, and I feel great!" I have not used this technique in my work; rather, I like to follow up the session by reinforcing what has been realized using other techniques,

---

107   www.soulcenteredtherapy.com/textfiles/**gestaltdreamwork**.htm

such as the TAT procedure.[108] For example, if an insight into a problem in a relationship has been gained, the negative affirmation might be: "This problem with . . . has happened." This is then followed by the positive affirmation: "This problem has been clarified, and I can relax now and am open to resolving the difficulty with ...."
Then the rest of the TAT procedure can be used. This can be found in the references cited.

The synthesis of the dream, relayed by the container, is usually the last step of the dream analysis.

Dialoguing

Three general types of dialoguing may be used during the analysis. You, the helper, can initiate these dialogues. These are between (1) you and the dream teller, (2) you and the dream part, and (3) the dream teller and the dream part.

I like to address the dream teller by name to distinguish between when I am addressing them as the dreamer versus the dream part; in the latter case, I will use the name of the character, and if not told the character's name, I will usually ask for that character's name. If addressing a nonhuman part of the dream, I may say something like: "Wedding cake, would you tell me about your experiences of when you were knocked off the table and fell to the floor?" If I forget to name who or what I am talking to, the dreamer might get confused as to whom or what they are giving voice.

In step 5 of the process, I will ask the dreamer to become a particular part of the dream. When the dreamer starts speaking as the particular part of the dream, I like to get acquainted with the part, getting the name, how the character (or object) knows the dreamer, etc. Then I may ask some specific questions, such as: "How are you related to the bride and groom or to (the dreamer's name)?" The answer may invoke other questions: "Do you know why the wedding

---

108   www.TATLife.com describes the acupressure points used and the outline of the way the affirmations are expressed. Also see Tapas Fleming, *TAT Professionals' Manual* (TAT Life Enhancement Series, 2007).

cake ended up on the floor?" Often I ask: "Do you have anything you want to say to (the dreamer's name)?" If a response follows, then I ask the dreamer to return to being the dreamer and responding to what the dream part just said. There may be several rounds of responses between the dreamer and the part, continuing until the conversation seems finished. Sometimes, something else comes up later in the dream, requiring the dreamer and the part to resume the dialog. At other times, I may become a part of the conversation, making it into a three-way discussion. Always, I need to make sure that everyone knows exactly who is speaking so that the process doesn't become confusing. Usually it is you, the helper, who suggests that voice be given to another part of the dream, but the dreamer may say, "_____ needs to speak next." So the dreamer is invited to become this new part.

Withholds.[109] The idea of withholds is valuable for the dream helper to keep in mind. A withhold is something that you have not said to someone or have withheld because you believe that it would be uncomfortable or excessively difficult to talk about. The withhold then becomes a barrier between you and the person with whom you have a withhold and limits your relationship with that person. People with whom you have a withhold are likely to appear as a character in your dreams. Your subconscious often desires to be relieved of the tension created by the withhold. This may be the reason for the appearance of this person in the dream.

Thus when you are helping someone else, it is wise to keep in mind that the dreamer may have a withhold with a character in the dream. You can initiate resolution of this tension by saying to the dreamer: "Is there something you have been avoiding saying to this person that you would like to say now?" If the answer is *yes*, then you facilitate the dialog between the two. I have seen real-life friendships mended as a result of using this process in a dream analysis.

---

109   This concept comes from the Living Essence teachings. *www.livingessence.com*

__Ethereal Plane Communication (EPC).__[110] Ethereal plane communication (EPC) is a conversation between a real person (in this case, the dreamer) and the higher self of another person (anybody in the dream, dead or alive). The other person may be a parent, friend, lover, etc. who appears in the dream. When using EPC, the person to whom you are speaking can be assumed to be that person's higher self. This can make difficult conversations much easier to initiate and carry out as the person's higher self is assumed to be above his or her ego pettiness and thus less defensive, vindictive, and judgmental. Sometimes, both the regular self and the higher self of the dream character can be engaged in dialogue. In the dream about the new house in which the prior owner's clothes had been left in the closet, first there was a dialogue with the prior owner. The dreamer then realized that she wanted to talk with the higher self of this prior owner. This dialogue proved to be very powerful and informative. If the dreamer is familiar with withholds and EPC, this familiarity facilitates the dream analysis. However, the work can go well without this prior knowledge and without the use of these words.

In the wedding dream, the dreamer had been at odds with her mother and had not spoken with her in many years. After the dialogue in the dream between mother and daughter, old hurts were understood and forgiven. A few days after the dream analysis, the dreamer called her mother. They had a good telephone conversation, and the two became good friends once again, with the mother actually coming to live with her daughter for a while to help her out with the arrival of her newborn son.

Finishing the Dream Analysis

As the helper, you may assume that some part or character in the dream has been able to assimilate the words of the various voices and obtain an overall understanding of the dream—the Gestalt of the dream. Often, this is the container of the dream, such as the room,

---

110   Ethereal Plane Communication (EPC) is another concept taught to Living Essence students.

the house, the field, etc. in which the dream took place. But at other times, this may be one of the characters or objects in the dream. It could even be something that did not even appear in the dream, such as the tarot card (as in the previous example).

When all the various viewpoints expressed in the dream have been told, then you instruct the dreamer to give voice to the container, as explained in chapter I. Usually you will clearly recognize the container, but the dreamer might also—if so, you should go with the dreamer's suggestion. After you ask the dreamer to become and give voice to the container, you can give instructions to the container by reminding that point of view that we are able to witness everything that happened in the dream, and thus everything in the dream can be explained to the dreamer. So you ask the container to explain why the dreamer had this dream at this time.

After the dream is explained, you can ask the dreamer whether something remains to be done to finish off the dream analysis. If there is something, then you keep going. This rarely happens.

If necessary, after concluding the dream, you can use a technique from hypnotherapy to bring the dreamer back into ordinary reality. Do this if the dreamer still has his or her eyes closed. You say: "I will count to five, and on the count of five, you will be back to ordinary reality." The process goes like this:

"One, you can begin to experience yourself lying here on the couch (or sitting in the chair), feeling yourself breathe.

"Two, you can take a deep breath now.

"Three, you can begin wiggling your toes and moving your hands.

"Four, you can stretch if you want to." (I usually stretch also.)

"And five, you can open you eyes now returning to (give time and date.)"

Conclusions

In the 1970s, in the Encounter Movement, Gestalt dream analysis was used as one of the encounter techniques derived from Gestalt therapy. It then became incorporated into Alchemical Hypnotherapy, which is Gestalt therapy under hypnosis. Hypnotic dream work has become a standard tool of hypnotherapists.[III] The technique presented here is not much different from the original method. It is done with or without the dreamer being in a hypnotic trance. The dream teller may go into light trance spontaneously or may simply stay awake. Sometimes in working with a new dreamer who has difficulty relaxing and getting into the dream, doing the first few dreams using formal hypnotic induction first can be helpful, but this is not usually necessary.

The benefits are:
I.   increased self-understanding,
II.   resolution of real-life problems, such a resolving a difficulty in a relationship with a friend or relative,
III.   gaining power from characters or symbols in the dream,
IV.   discovering the power of being in the present moment,
V.   getting more deeply into the creative potential of your subconscious, and
VI.   discovering that you can achieve a great analysis by having a Gestalt experience and without having to think too much about it.

Before beginning, it is suggested that both the dreamer and the helper read this to become more familiar with the technique.

III   Randall Churchill: *Become the Dream: The Transforming Power of Hypnotic Dreamwork* (Santa Rosa, CA: Transforming Press, 1997).

Acknowledgements

Virginia Speaks:

Rumi said that all experiences in life bring us to this place, but I especially and most importantly thank my friend, teacher, companion and adventurer on this path, Buck Rhodes. My life is filled with wonder and magic, and I am so grateful for you, and I love you, my dear friend. My two children have been my friends and supporters for many years, you are so loved, Josh and Jen. To my spiritual guides, teachers and friends who were with me at the ritual, Wren, Penn, Stephani and Leeza, all my blessings for you, as you have blessed my life greatly. To the Oneness Community of New Mexico, you are a continual source of love, inspiration and joy, and you are family. And of course to God, Goddess, Divine Consciousness, Creator, Great Spirit, and Sri AmmaBhagavan......thank you for being us.

Buck Speaks:

A major turnkey allowing me to go on this journey was the Oneness teaching of Bhagavan of the Oneness University in India. This key unlocked my mind allowing me to explore non-duality which in turn unlocked sacred literature's real teachings. Yet without

Virginia as co-adventurer this wouldn't have happened either. What an amazing soul you are Virginia. I've learned so much from you and without your participation in this adventure, it wouldn't have happened. This has truly changed my life and I've loved watching your life change too.

Also many others have contributed to the work. Gurubhai Khalsa who has been meditating with me for many years now has especially helped me to understand the role of the twelve disciples in my life and in the life of Jesus. Oz Anderson provided the encouragement, space and inspiration to keep me motivated with the writing part of this adventure. Many others have made contributions and inspiration especially Hunter Flournoy, Janice, and those who agreed to review our manuscript. Dr. Wilfrid Koponen edited our raw manuscript with many important suggestions.

From the Spirit World Jesus has so often made his presence felt and heard as has Nanak, the first Sikh guru. Bhagavan, though still living, has also provided inspiration and guidance from the spiritual plane.

Index

Made in the USA ———
Lexington, KY
11 February 2011